P9-DUA-800

INVENTING *the* SOUTHWEST

DATE DUE

DEMCO 38-296

INDIAN BUILDING
ALBUQUERQUE, NEW MEXICO

INVENTING *the* SOUTHWEST

THE FRED HARVEY COMPANY AND NATIVE AMERICAN ART

by **KATHLEEN L. HOWARD** *and* **DIANA F. PARDUE**

in cooperation with the **HEARD·MUSEUM**

foreword by **MARTIN SULLIVAN**

NORTHLAND PUBLISHING

Riverside Community College
Library
4800 Magnolia Avenue
Riverside, California 92506

MAY '97

E 98 .A7 H77 1996

Howard, Kathleen L.

Inventing the Southwest

Text type was set in Deepdene

Designed by Julie Sullivan,
Sullivan Scully Design Group

Cover design by Patrick O'Dell

Edited by Stephanie Morrison

Production supervised by Lisa Brownfield

Manufactured in Hong Kong
by South Sea International Press Ltd.

Copyright © 1996 by The Heard Museum
ALL RIGHTS RESERVED.

This book may not be reproduced in whole or in
part, by any means (with the exception of short
quotes for the purpose of review), without permission of the publisher. For information, address
Northland Publishing Company, P. O. Box 1389,
Flagstaff, AZ 86002-1389.

FIRST IMPRESSION
ISBN 0-87358-649-2

Library of Congress Catalog Card Number 95-49748
Library of Congress Cataloging-in-Publication Data
Howard, Kathleen, 1941-
    Inventing the Southwest : the Fred Harvey
    Company and Native American art / by
    Kathleen L. Howard and Diana Pardue.
        p.   cm.
    Includes bibliographical references and index.
    ISBN 0-87358-649-2 (sc)
    1. Indian art—Southwest, New—History.
    2. Pueblo art—History. 3. Fred Harvey
    (Firm)—History. 4. Atchison, Topeka, and
    Santa Fe Railway Company—History. 5.
    Tourist trade—Southwest, New—History. I.
    Pardue, Diana R. II. Title.
    E98.A7H77 1996
    704'.0397079259—dc20   95-49748

0595/7.5M/5-96

All photographs © the Heard Museum, Phoenix,
Arizona, unless otherwise specified as follows.
Heard Museum object photos by Craig Smith.

Dimensions in captions refer to height or length
unless otherwise specified. When two dimensions are
given, they refer to height x width.

The Albuquerque Museum: 78; *American Indian Art
Magazine:* frontispiece, contents (postcard), 89, 94,
95, 96 (both), 106; American Museum of Natural
History: 65 (poncho, catalogue number 50/9360),
69 (catalogue numbers 50/9310, 50/9314, 50/9431,
50/9526, 50/9547, 50/9613, 50/9646); Karen
Bartlett/Alvina Zimmerman: 103; The Brooklyn
Museum Archives, Culin Archival Collections.
Expeditions [2.1], Report on a Collection Trip
Among the Indians of New Mexico and California,
May-September 1907, page 212a, photograph of Dr.
George A. Dorsey, William Jones, and James R.
Murie: 28; Carnegie Museum of Natural History,
Pittsburgh, Pennsylvania: 28 (moccasins), 29
(parfleche); The Centennial Museum, the University
of Texas at El Paso, 14 (photograph by Ben Wittick);
Denver Art Museum, 23; Field Museum of Natural
History, Chicago: 29 (baskets, catalogue numbers
87743, 88745, 87758, 87764), 53 (Chemehuevi bas-
kets, catalogue numbers 103441 and 103440);
Framer's Workshop: xii (Railway pass); Grace
Hudson Museum, City of Ukiah, California: 30, 33,
62; Kathleen L. and William G. Howard: 64, 79, 82,
84, 87, 92 (both), 97 (pin); Hubbell's Trading Post
National Historic Site: 38, 46; The Henry E.
Huntington Library, San Marino, California: vi, 85,
107; Kansas State Historical Society: 13, 15, 66, 68, 81;
Library of Congress: 60 (Elle), 61 (Tom); Gregory
Lonewolf: xiv, 2 (Mildred), 24 (Juana), 123, 124, 126
(Gregorita), 132; Mesa Verde National Park Museum:
105 (pendant), 109 (bowl); Caryll and William
Mingst, Moose, Wyoming: 130; Museum of

Northern Arizona: 97 (bottom two), 112, 117, 129;
Museum of New Mexico, 12, 16, 25 (Indian
Building), 75; National Archives and Records
Administration: 61 (Tom and Elle); National
Museum of the American Indian, Smithsonian
Institution: 21, 135; Natural History Museum of
Los Angeles County: 20 (both variants); Nemesis
Productions, *Mary Jane Colter: House Made of
Dawn,* from the Stewart Harvey Family Collection:
11 (Minnie); The Nelson-Atkins Museum of Art,
Kansas City, Missouri, (Purchase: Nelson Trust),
xv, 11 (jar), 17 (Rosary and Guadalupe), 19, 20
(second phase), 27 (hat), 31, 49, 111; Old Trails
Museum, Winslow, Arizona: 86; Private
Collection: 109 (brochure); Raton Museum,
Raton, New Mexico: 121 (watercolor); Santa Fe
Railway: xi, 71 (ad), 88, 102; Owen Seumptewa:
105 (Paul); Southwest Museum: viii (photograph
by F. H. Maude); Tafoya Family Collection: 123;
Diane Thomas: 122, 125; University of Nevada, Las
Vegas, Helen J. Stewart Collection: 52; The
University of Arizona Library, Special Collections,
8, 22, 70 (both), 72, 73, 77, 110, 115.

Frontispiece (ii): Postcard of Elle and Tom of
Ganado in front of the Fred Harvey Company
Indian Building in Albuquerque, New Mexico,
c. 1910.

Title page (iii): Playing card produced by the Fred
Harvey Company in 1911. Only the Navajo weaver
Elle of Ganado and Hopi-Tewa potter Nampeyo
were mentioned by name.

Page vi: Pomo basketweaver Mary Benson, early
1900s

Contents (vii), top left: Fred Harvey, 1889;
top right: Pomo headdress, 8" (diameter of ring),
c. 1900; bottom left, 1903 postcard of Isleta Pueblo
woman; bottom right: San Ildefonso jar by Tonita
Pena or Marianita Roybal, 10", c. 1920

For Bill, Robert, and Carrie; in memory
of Herman, who started it all.
—K.L.H.

For Dan and Monica Miller; and to Byron Harvey III,
who understood the importance
of the Fred Harvey Collection and the significance
of the associated archival documents.
—D.F.P.

TABLE of CONTENTS

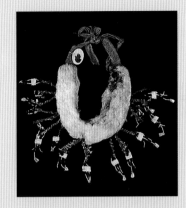

FOREWORD

◇

I n this hand-tinted photograph, a Santa Fe Railway train pauses to take on water during a desert stop in New Mexico. Passengers step off or lean through open windows to examine the fruit, vegetables, and hand-crafted pottery offered for sale by Pueblo families who have gathered from their nearby homes.

This single scene suggests the many transformations in American life that occurred around the turn of the twentieth century. It was the height of the railroad era. Here is the train itself, no longer a novelty, now a reliable scheduled link between the great cities of both coasts, its rails honeycombing the continent's once-remote interior reaches. Here are the passengers, men and women in the vanguard of the burgeoning middle class, travelers on business or in search of leisurely adventure. And here are the Pueblo people, residents of ancient and long-isolated farming communities, coming now into daily contact with the cash economy of urban-industrial America.

The Fred Harvey Company and the Santa Fe Railway joined forces at an auspicious historical moment. Borrowing new techniques in marketing and advertising, the companies promoted the American Southwest as an exotic destination. The railroad, the travelers, and the indigenous communities of the region were all integral elements in a partnership that spanned more than three-quarters of a century.

Women selling pottery to Santa Fe Railway
passengers at Isleta Pueblo in the early 1900s

OPPOSITE
Laguna Pueblo potters, late 1800s

*Santa Fe Railway trains in
Los Angeles, 1920s*

The first transcontinental railroad line was completed in 1869. By the 1890s, railroads had become the largest employers in the United States, the greatest consumers of iron, steel, and coal from the nation's industrial plants, and the most efficient and extensive movers of people and products in the history of the world. Despite sporadic depressions and business failures, railroads dominated every aspect of production and consumption in the American economy.

> *When my father's birthday was recorded the only way they could tell when a child is born [was] some important incident happened. That was the year the Santa Fe Railroad came through . . . 1884.*
> —WAYNE A. DALEY, SR., *Paraje, Age 77, 1995*

The growth of the railroad industry led to new forms of standardization and government regulation. Standard gauge rails and uniform routing and traffic procedures were steps toward forging a national rail network. By 1883, over the objections of towns that had always set their own local time by the sun, the railroads adopted uniform time zones (Standard Railway Time) throughout the continent. Passengers and freight shippers no longer had to guess what time to be at the station, or how to coordinate transfers. Henceforward, all Americans would keep time with the railroads. The Interstate Commerce Commission was created in 1887, the first of a long line of federal regulatory agencies, partly in response to pleas from the railroads themselves to impose order and fair competitive practices on the sprawling new industry.

By that time the Santa Fe Railway was competing for trade between Chicago and the West Coast with the more mature Union Pacific and Northern Pacific routes. Established in 1863 after Congress granted three million acres to help finance its construction, the Santa Fe struggled through difficult Colorado and New Mexico terrain, as well as several reorganizations, before it emerged from the depression of 1893 as a major line.

The railroad was America's most striking symbol of mobility. By 1910, there were 140,000 train stations dotting the landscape, and 95 percent of the nation's population lived near a station. Chicago was the hub of the iron corridors. In those days, a train departed from or arrived at Chicago's Union Station every four minutes. It was, and has remained, impossible to travel from the Northeast to the West Coast without changing trains in Chicago, so almost all the national railroads maintained offices there.

The Santa Fe Railway, like its competitors, pursued business through a series of rate wars that lowered the passenger fare from Chicago to the West Coast to as little as fifteen dollars during the 1890s, though it stabilized at fifty dollars for a round-trip ticket by the start of the new century.

Who were the travelers of that era? Many were recent immigrants from Europe, making a slow journey westward on hard board seats in overcrowded, crude coaches. Others, like the majority of passengers on the Santa Fe's lines through the Southwest, represented the nation's emerging urban middle classes. Beneficiaries of the post-Civil War consumer economy, they were the audience to whom the Santa Fe Railway and the Fred Harvey Company directed a torrent of imaginative new advertising.

Mobility, both social and geographic, became the hallmark of the middle classes. To be on the move was to move up. After the Civil War, the growth of enormous commercial, industrial, and mercantile businesses, aided by inventions like the typewriter and telephone, created a national demand for office workers, accountants, timekeepers, retail clerks, managers, and service staff of all kinds.

Santa Fe Railway advertisements drew images from Native American life as early as the 1890s. This advertisement appeared in the May 1902 issue of Country Life in America.

Santa Fe Railway dining car, 1925

1897 Atchison, Topeka, &
Santa Fe Railway pass

RIGHT
Santa Fe Railway dining car interior, c. 1890

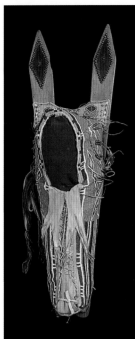

Kiowa beaded cradleboard, late 1800s

With the railroad, people could move where the jobs were. Cities that managed to snare major rail facilities drew new businesses and thousands of new residents instantly. Women moved to new employment outside the home as telephonists, typewriter operators, and department store sales clerks. Salaried workers of both sexes, busy on the job six days a week, moved up the social ladder by purchasing new consumer goods and services: factory-made clothing for both office and home, domestic furnishings and appliances, prepared foods, and leisure goods such as musical instruments, bicycles, cameras, and books. Urbanites crowded the lavish displays of such department stores as Wanamaker's, Macy's, and Marshall Field to sample these well-advertised products. Small town and rural residents enjoyed an equally ample market through the fat new Sears Roebuck and Montgomery Ward catalogues, as well as the inauguration of Rural Free Delivery in 1896 under Postmaster General John Wanamaker of department store fame. Wherever people lived, it was the railroad network that made possible an unprecedented access to consumer goods.

The railroad changed everyday life for Native Americans, too, but in less welcome ways. Rail lines sliced through the primeval grazing grounds of the Plains, bisecting traditional hunting routes and violating the boundaries of treaty land. Trains brought would-be settlers who were eager to try their luck on the patchwork of land grants made by the federal government as inducements to the railroad companies. At the same time, Congress passed the Dawes Act of 1887, which was intended to curtail the reservation system through individual land allotments to Native Americans.

Laguna water jar, 10", c. 1900

There was a depot here and the train used to stop. . . . People would sell fruit, potteries, and whatever souvenirs they had. The men would also try to sell corn, chili, whatever they planted. See, sometimes people would get out and sometimes they wouldn't and so we would go from one box [passenger car] to another selling through the window. . . . It helped the people in the pueblo.
—ANITA ABEITA,
age 82, Isleta Pueblo, 1994

Pueblo communities in New Mexico and Arizona, long reliant on a village-based agricultural economy, were less disrupted than their nomadic Plains and Apache neighbors. However, they too were affected. New Mexico's population tripled between 1880 and 1920, with new ranches and farms crowding ever closer to Pueblo lands. The Santa Fe Railway's tracks ran directly through Laguna Pueblo, forcing on its population an intimate daily encounter with the outside world. The tracks brought opportunity, too, as many Laguna residents found jobs in the maintenance and service departments of the Santa Fe. All communities were affected by the same profusion of new consumer goods that changed the lives of other Americans. Factory-made woolen and cotton goods, utensils, foodstuffs, and other conveniences led to inevitable changes, including a need for cash in order to acquire these goods.

By the turn of the century, many observers were convinced that Native American traditional cultures would not survive in the face of all these changes. Plains hunters on horseback now were tame objects of curiosity at Buffalo Bill Cody's railroad-borne Wild West shows as they toured the United States and Europe. Sculptors like Cyrus Dallin, Gutzon Borglum, and James Earle Fraser memorialized the vanquished warriors in monuments erected in urban parks and fairgrounds throughout the East and Midwest. With few exceptions, American Indians seemed consigned to a mythic past.

—MARTIN SULLIVAN, *Director, the Heard Musuem*

Woman's manta made of bayetta wool, c. 1865–1875

CHAPTER 1

FRED HARVEY
and the AMERICAN WEST

"Perhaps more than any single organization, the Fred Harvey System introduced America to Americans."
—FRANK WATERS, Masked Gods, 1950

Fred Harvey, 1889

OPPOSITE
Fred Harvey opened his first railroad restaurant in Topeka, Kansas, in 1876.

In 1850, thousands of European immigrants sought new homes and new lives in the United States. Among them was Frederick Henry Harvey. Arriving from England at the age of fifteen, Harvey initially worked as a dishwasher but later created the first chain of restaurants and railroad hotels in the United States. Harvey was the epitome of the Victorian era's self-made man, an entrepreneur who developed a distinctive niche in the growing consumer economy.

In 1876, Harvey shook hands with representatives from the Atchison, Topeka, & Santa Fe Railway, and began a working relationship to provide food service for railroad passengers. His restaurant was located at the depot in Topeka, Kansas. At a time when most railroad food was poor and inedible, Fred Harvey provided appetizing meals in comfortable dining quarters. His business grew quickly over the next two decades, aided by a good business reputation and the active help of the railroad in transporting employees, foodstuffs, produce, and other supplies at no charge.

1

The Fred Harvey girls were
so beautiful with the starched
white aprons, the long aprons,
the uniforms. They were so
pretty. I used to say, "Oh,
I'd like to grow up and be
a Fred Harvey girl". . . .
I always admired them
because they always looked
so nice, so neat, so starched,
so perfect.
—MILDRED PRADT,
Laguna Pueblo, Age 77, 1995

ABOVE RIGHT
Harvey girls, Sommerville, Texas, c. 1910

Fred Harvey hired young, single women from throughout the East and the Midwest
to serve as waitresses. The presence of the "Harvey girls" provided the assurance of a safe
environment that the Harvey Company and the Santa Fe Railway needed to entice
tourists to travel West. At the same time, images of Native Americans used in advertisements promised the traveler an element of adventure.

Fred Harvey's restaurant business coincided with dramatic changes in a growing
America. At the close of the nineteenth century, eastern American cities were becoming
intensely industrialized while the vast lands of the West were rapidly becoming fenced
and domesticated. Native Americans living in the East had been driven farther and farther west by a growing American population that included increasing numbers of
immigrants from Europe. Those Native Americans living in the West saw natural

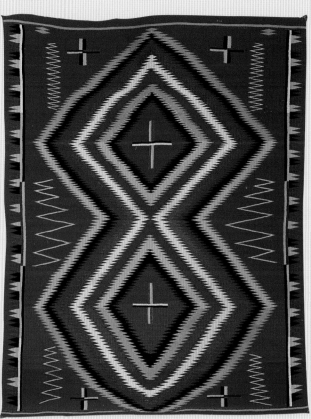

Navajo eyedazzler textile, 72" x 58", c. 1885

LEFT
Navajo Germantown pictorial textile, 49" x 29", c. 1885

OPPOSITE
Although miniaturized for the tourist market, these Pima baskets, 3"–6" diameter, early 1900s, were finely woven and exquisitely made.

Fred Harvey girl inlay figure by Leo Poblano, Zuni Pueblo, 5 3/4", c. 1948. It was given to Byron Harvey III by trader C.G. Wallace.

resources, which included abundant plant and animal life, greatly diminished as more Euro-Americans moved westward and fur trappers depleted available food sources. Struggles over land and resources resulted not only in the loss of life, but also in the restriction of Native Americans to reservations, many of which offered none of the self-sustaining resources that were the foundation of Native American life.

> *I remember we used to play in the tracks. I also remember that we'd hear the whistle 'cause we lived not too far from the railroad tracks. The conductor would toot his horn coming way over there. . . . And we'd go running and the conductor would throw out candy.*
> —RINA SWENTZELL, *Santa Clara Pueblo, Age 56, 1995*

Consequently, Native Americans were faced with the need to participate in the cash economy prevalent within the Euro-American population. At the same time, the railroad opened once-isolated Native American communities to regular contact with the contemporary consumer world. Native American groups located near railroad stops found a market for the pottery, basketry, and beadwork they produced. The Santa Fe Railway passed through Laguna Pueblo, a daily stop, some of whose residents found long-term employment as railroad laborers. Native Americans migrated as far as Richmond, California, where a Laguna community of many families flourished for decades, and to smaller southwestern communities such as Winslow, Arizona. Many returned to their Pueblo homes after retiring from railroad work. The infusion of cash earned from the sale of craft items and art altered the internal economies of communities that had relied on traditional subsistence ways of life.

Americans, escaping the noise and congestion of the cities and seeking adventure, traveled west by train in large numbers. Middle-income Americans enjoyed the luxury of seeing different lands and people without traveling abroad and the Santa Fe Railroad encouraged rail travel in advertisements that capitalized upon images of Native Americans.

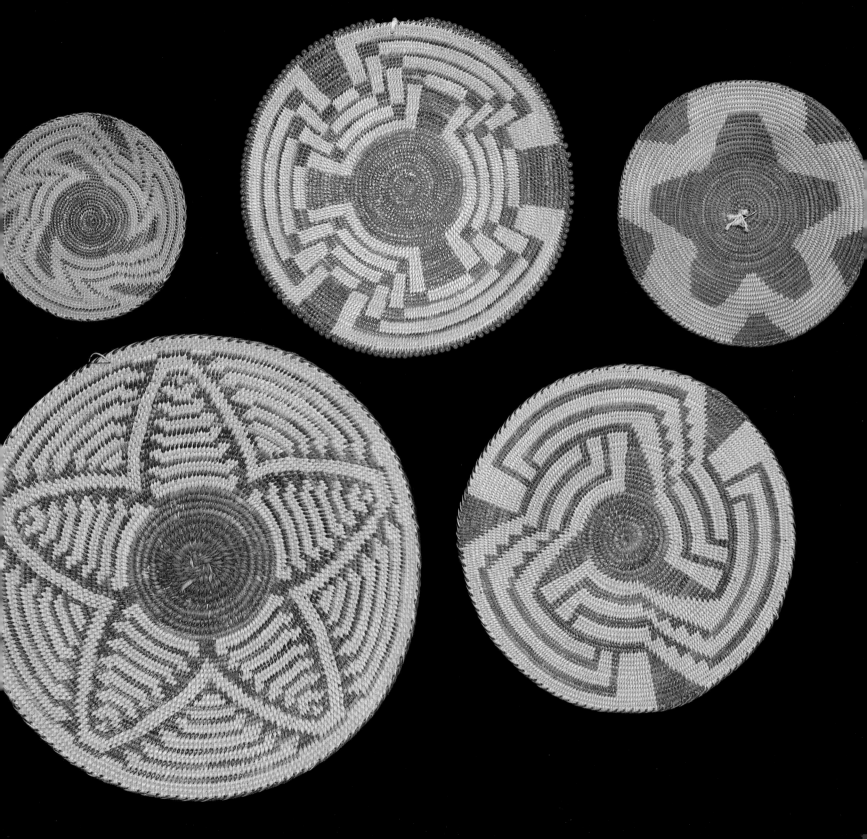

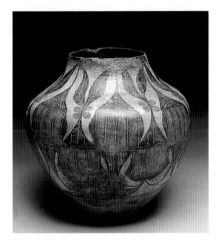

Depictions of Native Americans were used to promote travel on the California Limited in a number of national magazines in the 1890s.

Rail travelers prized the handmade traditional items they purchased at station stops, not only as mementos of their travel, but also as home decor popularized during the Arts and Crafts Movement of the late 1800s in Europe and the U.S. Repelled by mass-made and frequently inferior industrial products, and by the noise and grime of urban industrial life, arts and crafts devotees found not just beauty but virtue in indigenous craft arts:

The model home of the period contained clay vessels, embroidered textiles, stained-glass windows, metal lamps, and wood furniture. . . . The floors and walls, each piece of furniture, and every accessory provided opportunities to promote aesthetic and moral ideals. Proto-typical room settings . . . often included kindred objects made by or influenced by Native American, Asian American, African American, and Mexican American artists.
—LESLIE GREEN BOWMAN, American Arts and Crafts: Virtue in Design, 1990

Native American craft arts reflected the Victorian era interest in handmade objects and the rejection of industrialization. As traditional arts such as basketry, pottery, and textiles underwent a transition from utilitarian household objects to souvenirs and home decor, the materials and processes used to make the objects remained the same but their shapes and styles evolved. Many objects became miniaturized or simplified as they were made for sale. Forms such as basketry wastebaskets and pottery teapots were made for the first time by Native peoples. An important new market was developing for these objects.

Yes, the tourists used to come out and then the train would wait. . . . I guess, the train would wait at the edge of the village there . . . and then the people got out and took pictures of different people.
—ELIZABETH ARKIE, Laguna Pueblo, Age 72, 1995

OPPOSITE
Yavapai women selling beaded necklaces in Phoenix, early 1900s; inset: Mohave beaded necklaces like this, 10", were collected by the Fred Harvey Company for the museum in Albuquerque. With tourism, beadwork changed to less elaborate forms.

LEFT
Zia water jar, 12 1/2", c. 1905

BELOW
Zia water jar, 12", c. 1870–1875. Objects made for home use were also sold to train travelers.

CHAPTER 2

THE INDIAN DEPARTMENT *and* MUSEUM

❖

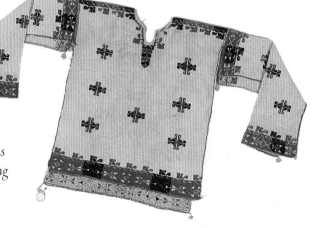

You are perhaps aware that this is not a purely commercial enterprise. Although it was intended to sell a greater part of our collections eventually, the first object in establishing this exhibit was to furnish an attraction for the Santa Fe [Railway] and I believe you realize it has been a most remarkable success in that direction.
—HERMAN SCHWEIZER TO WILLIAM RANDOLPH HEARST, *December 31, 1905*

Jemez shirt, 30" height, late 1800s

OPPOSITE
J. F. Huckel and Herman Schweizer in a Fred Harvey Company showroom, c. 1902–1904

By the time of his death in 1901, Fred Harvey's business included twenty-six restaurants, sixteen hotel/restaurants, and twenty dining cars on the Santa Fe Railway. The business Fred Harvey began and nurtured would continue to grow in the twentieth century as Harvey family members increased operations and extensively promoted tourist travel to the Southwest in conjunction with the Santa Fe Railway. After Fred Harvey's death, his son Ford took over the family-owned firm's operations. Minnie Harvey Huckel, Fred Harvey's daughter, proposed the idea of establishing a museum at The Alvarado Hotel in Albuquerque. With the support of Ford Harvey, her brother, and J. F. Huckel, her husband, plans were made to design and display ethnographic material in an elaborate craftsman-style museum. It had taken over five years to bring together the collections that were to be in the museum.

Four generations of Harvey family members:
Fred Harvey (portrait); left to right:
Byron Harvey, Sr., Byron Harvey III, and
Byron Harvey, Jr.

Known as the Fred Harvey Indian Department, the museum collections and sales rooms were initiated and overseen by J. F. Huckel. Huckel managed the Indian Department until his death in 1936, working closely with the main buyer for the company, Herman Schweizer. Schweizer, a German immigrant, was the central force in the development of the Indian Department.

Huckel, who lived in Kansas City, moved to Albuquerque to learn the business of buying and selling Native American–made objects from Schweizer. He was officially Schweizer's boss and head of the Indian Department, but in the Southwest, Schweizer was regarded as the "Harvey anthropologist" by writers, collectors, traders, and others.

Herman Schweizer's career had blossomed early in Harvey Company employ. During a September 1887 visit to the Harvey "eating house" in Coolidge, New Mexico (twenty miles east of present-day Gallup), Fred Harvey noted: "Coolidge: pastry poor, coffee poor, house generally poor." The company corrected this dismal situation by placing Schweizer, "one of the Harvey system's bright young men," in Coolidge to manage the lunch room when he was only sixteen. While working there, Schweizer began buying jewelry, blankets, and other objects from Navajo people and selling them to travelers passing through. In his free time, he rode horseback across the adjacent reservation lands and became acquainted with local people, Native American craftsmen, and Anglo traders. The network of friendships thus developed became the basis for his collecting activities and later led him to master the art of intriguing train travelers with Native American arts and crafts. Schweizer's small, successful business venture soon came to the attention of Minnie Harvey Huckel. The synergistic collaboration among Minnie Harvey Huckel, J. F. Huckel, and Herman Schweizer created the birth and advanced the growth of the Fred Harvey Indian Department and established The Alvarado Hotel complex as the heart of the Southwest in the minds of tourists.

> *Where do I take my stand when I survey the Southwest? Not in coastal Malibu where I live, not in Los Angeles where I work; both are marginal vantage points, as were Dobie's in Austin, Campbell's in Norman. It is at the heart that I take my stand; at the heart of hearts, the cor cordium, in Albuquerque, New Mexico, that ancient crossing of the Rio Grande.*

MINNIE HARVEY HUCKEL

MINNIE HARVEY HUCKEL was born in Leavenworth, Kansas, on July 1, 1871. One of five children born to Frederick Henry Harvey and Barbara Mattas Harvey, she attended Eastern schools and traveled extensively in Europe. On November 5, 1896, she married John Frederick Huckel and in 1898 they moved to Kansas City, Missouri.

Minnie became an ardent student and discriminating collector of Native American arts and crafts. Every year, she traveled by train and wagon to the Four Corners area to visit Pueblo and Navajo country. Her greatest interest was not in the country itself, but in its people.

It was Minnie's idea to start a museum of Southwestern arts and crafts in Albuquerque at The Alvarado Hotel. As Fred Harvey's daughter and J. F. Huckel's wife, she was assured support from company officials for her ideas, suggestions, and projects. She was friend and mentor to Mary Jane Colter, supporting her important position as architect in the company for over forty years. In 1902, she was on hand at The Alvarado Hotel in Albuquerque to assist Colter with the finishing touches on the interior decorations for the Indian Building and Museum. She also helped design the Harvey's Cardeñas Hotel in Trinidad, Colorado.

Minnie and J. F. Huckel collected 111 Navajo sandpaintings and other Indian objects. A Hopi jar, made by Nampeyo and collected by the Huckels, can be seen in the photo below.

The Huckel's maintained residences in Kansas City and at the Broadmoor at Colorado Springs.

After J. F. Huckel's death, Minnie Huckel became a director of the Fred Harvey Company and its principal stockholder. At her death, her niece, Katherine Harvey, donated the 111 Navajo sandpaintings documented by Gladys Reichard in *Navajo Medicine Man* to the Colorado Springs Fine Arts Museum.

This jar, made by Nampeyo, appears to be the one acquired by Huckel in the early 1900s and given to Katherine Harvey.

HERMAN SCHWEIZER

THE ELDEST OF SIX CHILDREN of Benzion Schweizer and Pauline Gundelfinger, Herman Schweizer was born August 10, 1871, in Eppingen, Baden, Germany. He arrived in New York City on September 12, 1885. From there, young Herman traveled to Chicago where he lived with relatives for six or seven months. He then moved on to Los Angeles, arriving with two dollars in his pocket. Over the next few years Herman moved around California, Arizona, and New Mexico doing whatever work he could get, mostly related to rail travel. He became a naturalized citizen on July 11, 1902. For a time he was a newsboy on Atlantic and Pacific Railroad trains.

By 1899 Schweizer was jobbing out turquoise and silver to Native American silversmiths through a trading post in Thoreau, New Mexico. He furnished silversmiths with lightweight silver and small turquoise stones and asked them to make jewelry that would appeal to tourists wanting souvenirs to take home. Schweizer rose to the position of Manager of the Fred Harvey Indian Department headquartered in Albuquerque, a position he held until his death on November 11, 1943.

Schweizer had a keen collector's eye for rare Indian art and his influence as master collector, buyer and seller of Indian art objects was well recognized in his day. Thirty-five years of correspondence, visits to San Simeon and business transactions with William Randolph Hearst testify to how desirable items in the Fred Harvey collection were to contemporary, wealthy collectors.

Schweizer was known as "the Harvey anthropologist" because of the great interest and knowledge he had acquired living and working among Indian people. Navajo people referred to him as *Hosteen Tsani* (bald-headed man).

Besides William Randolph Hearst, his correspondence reveals business relationships with Mary Austin, J. L. Hubbell, George Heye, George Dorsey, Jesse Nusbaum, and other individuals of national prominence. His letters indicate his involvement in staffing Albuquerque and Grand Canyon locations with Native American artist-demonstrators, some of whom worked for the company for forty years. He assisted with the staging of two world's fairs for the Fred Harvey Company and the Santa Fe Railway, one in San Francisco and one in San Diego.

In 1989, Sotheby's offered at auction a Navajo first phase chief blanket with a Herman Schweizer/Fred Harvey provenance. When the gavel finally dropped, the sale achieved a new world price record for a Native American art object: $522,000.

I will be even more precise and say just where it would be in Albuquerque: on the station platform of the Alvarado, one of the last of the Harvey Houses and the most beautiful of them all, old gray stucco with the turquoise trim, its cool courts and shady patios inviting siesta, its Indian museum packed with old Pueblo artifacts, its slow heartbeat the coming and going of the Santa Fe trains.

—Lawrence Clark Powell,
Southwestern Book Trails, 1963

The Indian Department began as a not-for-profit operation but soon took on a life of its own. As Herman Schweizer put it in a May 15, 1935 letter to C. E. Faris of the U.S. Indian Service:

I don't think it is necessary for me to call your attention to what we have been doing here at Albuquerque and the Grand Canyon for the last thirty years. Millions of people have been enabled to see Indians and Indian exhibits on their way through Albuquerque who would not otherwise have had this opportunity.

Also, it may interest you to know that the Santa Fe Railway, when this place was built, considered it first of all as an advertisement of the Southwest Indians and incidentally, of course, of the Santa Fe Railway, and the commercial part was only considered incidental.

In 1930, Schweizer wrote to Mary Austin, well-known Western author, to explain the purpose of the business endeavor:

Our place here was established thirty years ago on such a large scale, primarily as an advertising feature of the Santa Fe Railway, with a view of interesting the public in the Indians of

J. F. Huckel

John Frederick Huckel was born in New York in 1864. In 1885 he graduated from Williams College and went to work at the publishing firm of Harper and Brothers, now HarperCollins. Later he worked as an assistant publisher for the *New York Evening Post.* In 1896, he married Minnie Harvey, daughter of Fred Harvey. In 1898, the Huckels moved to Kansas City where J. F. Huckel joined the Fred Harvey Company. Huckel strongly felt that historic and aesthetic values should be joined with business development.

With the support of the Fred Harvey organization, Huckel established the Fred Harvey Company Indian Department. Huckel and Herman Schweizer worked as a team creating the museum in Albuquerque and collections of rare Native American and Hispanic art objects.

Huckel's obituary in the *Kansas City Times,* March 27, 1936, stated:

The design and planning of new Harvey hotels along the Santa Fe was left largely to his enthusiastic mind. He labored with architects in the scheming of buildings that would reflect Spanish and Indian backgrounds. Mr. Huckel went on to exemplify this style in the main towns along the Santa Fe. Arches, stucco and brick walls, beamed ceilings and Spanish furniture were part of this style.

The Alvarado Hotel, c. 1902

the Southwest and their products, which purpose has admittedly been well served, and it has not only been of great benefit to the Santa Fe Railway, but to the Indians and all dealers in these products, as when we entered the field there was established values on anything, and a blanket or basket was worth only what anyone could get for it.

The commercial side originally was a secondary consideration, as for commercial purposes along the Railway Company would not have consented to devote such a large space for such a purpose.

The major part of the Indian Building here was arranged in the form of exhibits, cozy corners, etc. to illustrate to people how these things can be utilized to best advantage.

Beckoned to an idyllic adventure, to a country within a country, travelers along the Santa Fe Railway line from Chicago to California visited the Alvarado and its adjacent Fred Harvey Indian Building. Surrounded by friendly Native American people who displayed and explained the wares available for sale, tourists stepped into an idealized world of virtual reality created for them by the Harvey Company. Most of them were smitten by what they saw and years after reflected on memories of a visit to what many thought of as the heart of the Southwest.

The birth of the Indian Department coincided with the opening of the Fred Harvey Company's Alvarado Hotel in Albuquerque on May 11, 1902. The account filled an entire page of the *Albuquerque Journal-Democrat*. Designed by Charles Whittlesey, Santa Fe Railway architect, the new hotel was the biggest and most elaborate building in Albuquerque. Newspapers touted the Alvarado as a "haven offering the weary rail

FORD FERGUSON HARVEY

BORN ON MARCH 7, 1866, in Leavenworth, Kansas, Ford Harvey was only ten years old when his father started the Fred Harvey restaurant business. He attended Racine College in Racine, Wisconsin, but gave up his college career in 1884 because of his father's failing health. When Fred Harvey died, Ford Harvey assumed leadership of the Harvey organization.

When Ford Harvey died on December 13, 1928, the company that bore his father's name stretched from the Great Lakes to the Gulf of Mexico and the Pacific Coast. At that time, the company had more than six thousand employees and was operating sixty hotels and dining facilities. Ford Harvey's obituary in the January 1929 issue of *The Santa Fe Magazine* stated:

While the original ideas of the founder were adhered to closely in his conduct of organization, Mr. Harvey and his partners introduced innovations and expansions the success of which have justified these departures.

The Southwest was Mr. Harvey's only real hobby, outside of building the business founded by his father. He was interested particularly in preserving the native country against the encroachments of modernization.

In the early 1900s, the Fred Harvey Company building at The Alvarado Hotel contained a room for objects from Mexico and northern New Mexico.

OPPOSITE
Left: Bulto of Our Lady of the Rosary, 31", by the Santo Nino Santero, Hispanic northern New Mexico, c. 1850; top right: Retablo of Our Lady of Guadalupe, 29", by the Laguna Santero, Hispanic northern New Mexico, c. 1796–1810; bottom right: Retablo of Saint Barbara, 31 1/2", by the Laguna Santero, Hispanic northern New Mexico, c. 1796–1810

traveler a respite from the exhaustion of train travel." History, legend, myth and purple prose came together in the company's 1904 brochure, *the Alvarado, a New Hotel at Albuquerque, New Mexico:*

> *A great, wide-spreading building, like a Spanish Mission save for its new-ness; rough, warm gray walls and a long procession of arches; all under a red tile roof with many towers—this, facing the distant purple mountains and set against the turquoise sky, is the Alvarado.*
> *. . . This hotel, with all its mechanical and artistic perfections, stands in America's most fascinating region—the Rio Grande valley. Back of it lies the thriving city of Albuquerque, and beyond that the Mexican old-town sleeps as it has slept for centuries. Before it, the valley, an oriental oasis in the desert, blooms and yields abundantly. And all about are tokens of the strenuous past.*

The brochure details the niceties of a hotel stay staged to perfection to give the tourist a complete Southwestern cultural experience without ever having to leave the hotel. The Harvey Company was successful in selling the comfort it had created. Collector, anthropologist, and consultant to the Harvey Indian Department, Dr. John Hudson, while an Alvarado guest, wrote to his wife, artist Grace Hudson on February 6, 1903:

> *My Dear Grace—I got here this a.m. just before daybreak and was given a room as hand-some and inviting as any in the land. The mattress was so extraordinarily soft that really I lay awake in the bliss of realization of perfect comfort.*

The next day Hudson wrote further:

> *Four or more long trains pass here daily and they never fail to take advantage of the half hour stop to run into this little gem of a hotel and seem just like wondering, delighted chil-dren and I don't blame them, for everything is quaint and comfortable to the last degree. In front of the big fireplaces are upholstered swings for four, swung by big chains from the ceil-ing and are delightful to sit in.*

The "Indian and Mexican Building and Museum" was described in the 1904 brochure as follows:

OPPOSITE
Navajo third phase chief blanket, 44" x 58",
c. 1880

At Albuquerque visitors will enjoy the unique Indian and Mexican Building and the Indian Museum. For five years the Harvey experts have been engaged in making the collections here displayed. Indian villages, buried cities, remote cliff dwellings, and isolated hogans have been searched for the rarest exponents of Indian life.

In the first-named building is an exhibit of the finest old Navajo blankets ever woven. While a specialty has been made of obtaining old Navaho patterns in native dyes and fine weaves—such as the priceless bayettas—the display of new blankets is a notable one....

In the half dozen rooms in the Indian and Mexican Building special collections of inestimable value have been grouped. No one can afford to pass by the superbly woven, gossamer shawls, the exquisitely drawn work, the old paintings, engravings, jewelry, weapons, and woodwork of the Spanish and Mexican Room. The Navajo Room, with its blanketed walls and decorations of pottery and basketry, furnishes an admirable idea for a luxurious home "den." A superb collection representing all the arts and customs of the South Seas has been separately installed.

In another room a summer hogan of the Navahos has been cunningly wrought, and there may be seen patient Navaho squaws weaving blankets; their men engaged in fashioning showy bracelets, rings and trinkets; Indians from Acoma, Laguna making pottery; skillful Pueblos plaiting baskets; and workers in hair, leather and cloth. Undisturbed by the eager gaze of the tourist, the stoic works on as unconcernedly as though in his reservation home. For these Indian workpeople, a model village is building on nearby ground.

The harmony of colors in the Indian and Mexican Building is marked. The goods are so artistically arranged and grouped that one first sees only the beautiful, symmetrical whole.

Panamint basket, 3" x 9" x 6", c. 1900

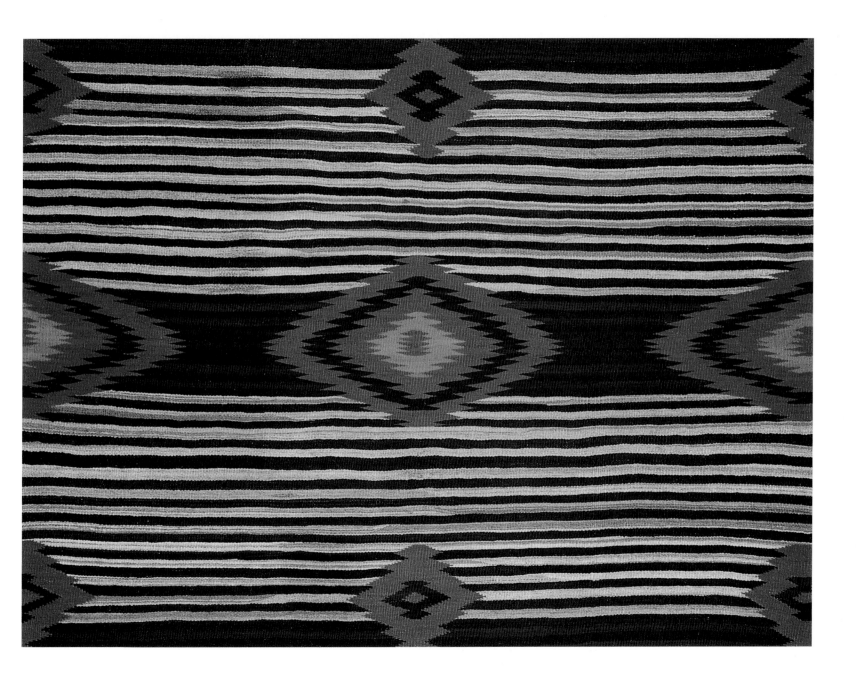

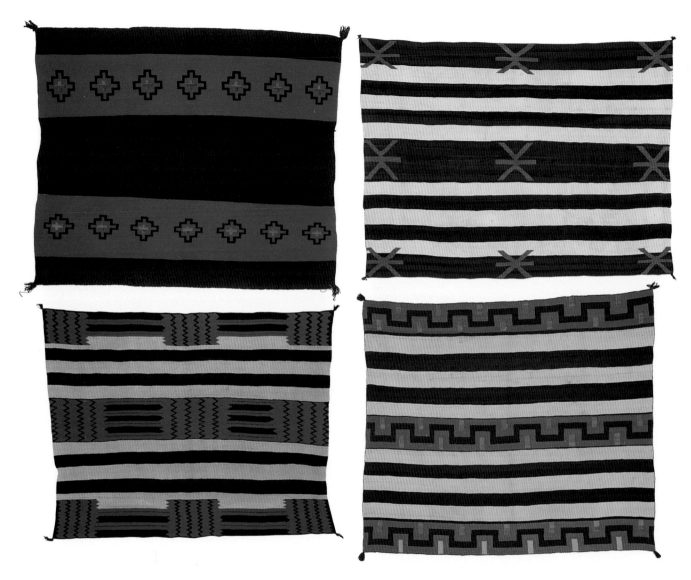

TOP LEFT: *Navajo manta or shawl, 46" x 59", c. 1865–1870. This was purchased from Mr. Andrus on January 20, 1902.*
TOP RIGHT: *Navajo second phase chief blanket, 52" x 71", c. 1860–1865.* BOTTOM LEFT: *Navajo chief blanket, second phase variant,*
54" x 73", c. 1870–1875. This was purchased by the Harvey Company on December 24, 1913, and later sold to William Randolph Hearst.
BOTTOM RIGHT: *Navajo chief blanket, variant, 55 1/2" x 65", c. 1875–1885. This blanket also belonged to William Randolph Hearst;*
he was a primary collector of textiles.

In the Collection Building [Museum] the articles and collections are arranged by a celebrated ethnologist, according to archaeological and anthropological bearing. Every product of every age is exhibited and classified. Money could not buy this magnificent display.

Much of the exhibit . . . may be purchased and the vaults and storehouses contain rich stores waiting to be brought to light.

As each train arrived in Albuquerque, passengers stepped from the train to the platform in front of the depot and Indian Building, which housed the Indian Department's museum, sales rooms, and artist/demonstrators. A retaining wall separated the tracks from the hotel grounds. Passengers could choose one of three sets of steps to reach the lower level where The Alvarado Hotel complex stood. It was not possible to get to the main hotel facilities without first passing the Indian Building: each set of steps directed passengers past it toward the lobby, dining room, and coffee shop. The Alvarado Hotel and Santa Fe Railway depot stretched seven hundred feet north to south along the railroad tracks. Gray stucco and turquoise-trimmed arches and towers surrounded cool, lush gardens highlighted by a pool and wall fountain.

It was like a palace. Everything was so pretty. They had so many Indian artifacts. It was just a beautiful place to be.
—MILDRED PRADT, *Laguna Pueblo, Age 77, 1995*

Santo Domingo jar, 7", and bowl, 11 1/2", by Monica Silva, early 1900s

ABOVE LEFT
Santo Domingo man selling pottery in front of the Fred Harvey Company Indian Building at The Alvarado Hotel, 1907

CHAPTER 3

BUYING *and* SELLING COLLECTIONS

This Kwakiutl mask, 15" x 24", hung on the interior wall of the Indian Building in Albuquerque.

OPPOSITE
Interior view of the Indian Building at The Alvarado Hotel in which the above Kwakiutl mask is visible

One of the representatives of the American Museum has stated that good material is disappearing among the pueblos and that they are going to get right in the field and get some before it was too late, and I am anxious that we should get what we want first.
—J. F. HUCKEL TO H. R. VOTH, *May 13, 1910*

Several months before the opening of The Alvarado Hotel in Albuquerque, the Fred Harvey Company had generated excitement by announcing the establishment of a large-scale museum to be housed at the site. The future museum was described as "the most extensive ethnological museum in the country" and "the largest and most complete of its kind in the world" (*Albuquerque Journal-Democrat*, March 7 and 1, 1902).

Huckel and Schweizer utilized several strategies to attract tourists to the Southwest and increase sales of the Native American objects they acquired; these included modeling the commercial business after a plan of exhibiting and selling cultures that had been successfully developed for world's fairs. The Harvey Company anthropology displays at many of the world's fairs, including the 1893 Field Columbian Exposition in Chicago, went to elaborate lengths to replicate the homes of select groups of Native peoples.

We used to clean all the things that were in the store inside [the Alvarado]. We used to get the potteries down and clean them and put them back, and when we get through with that, we start with the floors, clean them before the trains come in. And when they tell us a train is about to be here we used to quit so they wouldn't find us doing that, and after they take off we start over again.
—JUANA SANGRE, *age over 90, Isleta Pueblo, 1994*

Two factors were essential to duplicate the world's fair formula. Firstly, Huckel and Schweizer had to acquire major collections of Native American craft arts from traders, major private collectors, and entrepreneurs of the day. Secondly, they had to hire Native American artist-demonstrators to attract tourists to the Indian Department display room. Huckel and Schweizer successfully accomplished both goals but not without some difficulty.

Huckel and Schweizer began purchasing large collections of Native American craft arts prior to the opening of the Alvarado. Although positioned in the Southwest, the Indian Department focused on collections beyond that regional boundary and included objects made by diverse groups of Native Americans located west of the Mississippi. Collections of Native American–made objects were acquired from regions as far west as California and as far north as Alaska. Objects were sought both for display in the museum and for sale to a complex market.

Huckel and Schweizer employed many purchasing methods. They purchased large collections from traders and private collectors; this offered many advantages. In the formative years of the Indian Department, it was necessary to acquire stock rapidly and in large numbers in order to present a strong visual impression in the showroom. Also, the acquisition of well-known collections brought legitimacy to a newly developing business.

They also acquired extensive collections from ethnographers who traveled into Native American lands and purchased what became known among themselves and museums as "field collections." Field collections brought a level of legitimacy and authenticity sought by the Harvey Company for the newly formed museum as well. These collections were either retained at the museum in Albuquerque or marketed to natural history museums such as the Field Columbian Museum in Chicago, the Carnegie in Pittsburgh, and the Heye Foundation, now the Museum of the American Indian, in New York.

OPPOSITE
Tesuque jar, 11 1/2", c. 1890

LEFT
Interior of the Indian Building at The Alvarado Hotel in Albuquerque, c. 1905

This Pomo basket, 23", by Mary Benson, can be seen on the upper right shelf in the Indian Building at left.

In addition to collections, Huckel and Schweizer sought objects held by individuals. These generally consisted of old, rare articles that went into the museum initially or eventually become the property of a persistent collector.

From the onset the Harvey Company recognized the importance of collections to the future of the museum. These collections were described by the newspapers in terms of their "scientific value." Equally important to the company was the association with known curators and ethnologists, which was also reflected in newspaper coverage: "Indeed, in gathering and classification of the specimens, some of the best known scientists of the country have contributed" (*Albuquerque Journal-Democrat*, March 1, 1902).

The Harvey Company also sought to establish a reputation for authenticity and prestige by hiring eminent curators and ethnographers to build collections that would either be retained at the museum or sold to natural history museums throughout the country. The stated intent of the Harvey Company Indian Department was to create an attraction for the Santa Fe Railway, but in actuality, the Indian Department's business of selling ethnographic materials was a profitable enterprise for the company.

Tlingit basket, 12", c. 1900

In order to amass scientific collections, Huckel and Schweizer formed a key association with Dr. George A. Dorsey, the first individual to receive a doctorate in anthropology from a United States university, Harvard, and curator of anthropology at the Field Columbian Museum in Chicago. Already known to Schweizer by 1898, Dorsey took a partial leave of absence from the Field Museum from January 1903 through April 1904. Dorsey resided at The Alvarado Hotel in Albuquerque where he was employed by the Indian Department. Dorsey had conducted field work among the Arapaho and Osage for some time. He acquired collections from those cultures for the Indian Department, but otherwise his collecting activities on behalf of the Harvey Company seem somewhat vague.

Most importantly, Dorsey served as a resource for the Indian Department, connecting Huckel and Schweizer with field ethnographers and curators who became dually employed by the Field Museum and the Indian Department. The ethnographers included Mennonite missionary and Hopi ethnographer

Henrich R. Voth; assistant curator at the Field Museum and Southwest archaeologist and ethnographer Charles Owen; California ethnographer Dr. John Hudson; and Northwest ethnographer Dr. Charles F. Newcombe. So complex were the business arrangements of the dual employment that on at least one occasion Voth was confused as to the source of his salary. Voth wrote to D. C. Davies, recorder at the Field Museum on April 2, 1904:

> *In a previous communication I believe I wrote you that the Fred Harvey people would pay my salary while I am out here. From a letter received from Dr. Dorsey*

with today's mail, I see that I had misunderstood him. It seems he meant that the "expenses" for myself and stenographer would be paid by the Harvey people. As to the salary, he says, "The salary and the salary alone of yourself and your assistant is to be defrayed by the Field Columbian Museum."

George Dorsey was a significant figure in the developmental years of the Fred Harvey Company between 1903 and 1904, connecting the company to ethnologists of the day and lending his name and that of others to a premier collection of Native American–made objects. The Harvey Company capitalized on the working association, using the ethnographic research of Dorsey, Hudson, Voth, Owen, and others to catalogue the object collection and to develop books, brochures, and other printed material to entice visitors to the Southwest and to sell the object collections they had amassed. In the formative years of the Indian

San Ildefonso jar by Martina Vigil and Florentina Montoya, 11", 1905–1916

Haida hat, 14" diameter, late 1800s

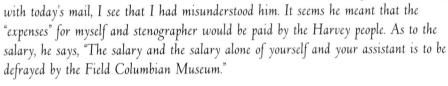

Dr. George A. Dorsey with Sauk and Fox consultant William Jones and Pawnee consultant James F. Murie, c. 1907

Arapaho moccasins, 10", collected by Dr. George Dorsey, c. 1900

Department, Huckel and Schweizer carefully commandeered publicity that positioned the museum at the Alvarado within the realm of science. The *Albuquerque Journal-Democrat* reported frequently on activities by ethnographers Dorsey, Hudson, and Voth at the Alvarado:

> *Dr. Hudson, the noted scientist of the Field Columbian museum, who has been here several days cataloguing the baskets of the Harvey collection, left for the west yesterday.* (February 11, 1903)

Other news reports validated and confirmed the scientific value of Indian Department collections and activities through the use of Dorsey's name:

DR. GEORGE A. DORSEY WRITES OF TREASURES IN FRED HARVEY COLLECTION
Dr. George A. Dorsey, curator of the department of ethnology in the Field Columbian museum whose research work in New Mexico has attracted wide attention in scientific circles throughout the world. (Albuquerque Journal-Democrat, September 26, 1903)

Brooklyn Museum curator Dr. Stewart Culin, a close associate of Dorsey, visited the Alvarado on one of his trips to the Southwest. Schweizer assisted Culin by making arrangements with John Lorenzo Hubbell, a trader at Ganado, Arizona, for a portion of Culin's trip. Local newspaper coverage emphasized the scientific nature of the research conducted by Culin and Schweizer as well as Culin's importance as an anthropologist. The *Albuquerque Journal-Democrat* article discussed Spanish swords and "rare old pottery" that was exhibited at the Field Columbian Exposition in Chicago in 1893 and later acquired by the Harvey Company:

> *When Dr. Stewart Culin, the great ethnologist was here the other day his attention was drawn to these swords. . . . Mr. Switzer and Dr. Culin, who are ferreting out the history of the blades, think it would well accord with the fitness of things if they could prove that Alvarado himself once owned them.* (April 2, 1903)

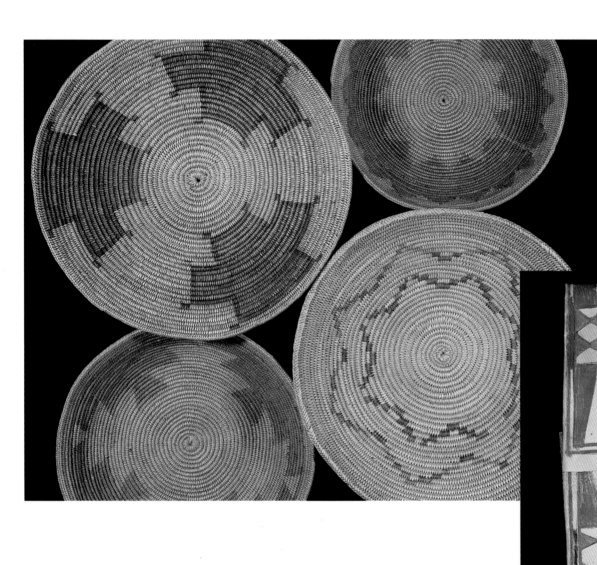

Navajo baskets, 10"–12", purchased by Dr. George Dorsey in 1904 from the Fred Harvey Company for the Field Museum in Chicago

Arapaho parfleche, 24", collected by George Dorsey, c. 1900

Dr. John Hudson, shown here with his wife, Grace Carpenter Hudson, collected material for George Dorsey of the Field Museum, Chicago, and for the Fred Harvey Company

The Fred Harvey Company acquired extensive collections of Native American material through associates of Dr. George Dorsey. One important individual who sold collections was collector and anthropologist Dr. John Hudson. A medical doctor by profession, Hudson amassed large collections of California basketry, which caught the attention of the Field Columbian Exposition committee members in 1893 in Chicago. Although this collection was sold to the Smithsonian, Hudson continued to build collections and subsequently sold another large collection to the Harvey Company in 1903. In 1903 and 1904 Hudson was working dually for the Indian Department and the Field Museum. Dorsey wrote to Hudson in Chicago, stating: "Desiring to meet you in Albuquerque please leave Chicago on Tuesday Feby 3d."

In February 1903, Hudson traveled to Albuquerque to unpack and display his collection as well as a collection from his mother-in-law, Helen Carpenter. Hudson wrote to his wife of the activities: "Mothers baskets will arrive tonight so I will be busy tomorrow with them probably. Both [collections] are to be segregated into groups of sale baskets, f.c.m. [Field Columbian Museum] specimens & Albuquerque Museum specimens." Hudson remained for several days at the Alvarado to arrange a display of the Pomo basket collection in the Museum.

Hudson continued to work for the next year for both the Indian Department and the Field Museum gathering collections primarily from California. On occasion, Hudson was accompanied by Dorsey on the buying trips. The volume of material sought by the Harvey Company is perhaps best expressed in a letter from Dorsey to Hudson written on April 9, 1903, in which Dorsey instructs Hudson "to get into Hupa country":

By the way, while you are in there I wish you would gather together, if possible, two or three hundred of the decorative Hupa caps, to be used at Albuquerque. They should not cost over a dollar or a dollar and a half apiece. Get every good one that you can get hold of. Of course we shall not want any of these for the Museum, except perhaps a half dozen or a dozen, to show the different styles of decoration.

Hudson traveled into Hupa country and among the Klamath people as well. He wrote to his wife on September 18, 1903: "I really believe that four fifths of the people between here and Hupa know me and my mission. All along the line I was hailed and treated nicely."

Another important collector and field ethnographer linked by George Dorsey to the Fred Harvey Company was H. R. Voth. In the 1880s, Voth lived in the territory of Oklahoma working among the Cheyenne and Arapaho and he moved to live among the Hopi in 1893. Although his move was prompted by his career as a Mennonite missionary, Voth became an adept student of the Hopi language and a collector of a range of Hopi material, much of which was ceremonial in nature. Voth and Dorsey met in 1897 when Dorsey traveled through the Southwest on an expedition for the Field Museum.

As with Hudson, Voth's employment with the Harvey Company was arranged through Dorsey, and Voth received his instructions from Dorsey. Later, after Dorsey returned to full-time employment at the Field Museum, Voth corresponded directly with J. F. Huckel and Herman Schweizer.

Voth sold collections of Hopi ethnographic and ceremonial materials to the Harvey Company, and much of this material was displayed by the Harvey Company at the Louisiana Purchase Exposition in St. Louis in 1904. Among the masses of visitors attracted by the exposition were anthropologists. Participation in the

Hupa cap, 7" diameter, c. 1900

Pomo basket, 17 3/4" diameter, late 1800s.

RIGHT
Pomo basket, 16 3/4" diameter, c. 1900

OPPOSITE
*Many of the baskets hudson sold to
the Harvey Company can be seen in
photographs of his basket collection from the late
1800s.*

exhibition provided exposure for the Harvey Company collections, which were built not only for display in the museum in Albuquerque but also for sale to large natural history museums and private collectors.

Charles Owen, assistant curator at the Field Museum, was also instrumental in building collections of Hopi material for the Field Museum and the Fred Harvey Company. Owen served primarily as an archaeologist for the Field Museum excavating sites in proximity to various Hopi villages and shipping hundreds of boxes of artifacts to the Field Museum. He also collected White Mountain Apache material for the Fred Harvey Company, probably in 1903 or as much as a decade later. In 1911 and in 1913, Owen sold Hopi kachina dolls and ethnographic material to the Harvey Company.

The Indian Department's alliance with Dorsey resulted in the acquisition of large collections of Native American material accumulated by Hudson, Voth, Owen, and possibly others, which were later sold at considerable profit. At the turn of the century, competition for collections was intense among emerging natural history museums. The Indian Department served as both broker and puppeteer, pulling strings to buy and sell to relatively newly formed natural history museums seeking to fill gaps in their collections. Huckel expressed this sentiment to Voth when in 1910 he referred to the decline in availability of older material and the collecting interest of the American Museum of Natural History in New York.

Hudson Coll.

The Harvey Company was successful in selling collections to many natural history museums and Dorsey appears to have been instrumental in some of the sales. In his letter of introduction to James Mooney of the U.S. National Museum, now the Natural History Museum of the Smithsonian Institution, Huckel mentions Dorsey. Mooney initially purchased a shield for the National Museum and later, several baskets.

Dorsey, Hudson, and Voth provided other services for the Harvey Company in addition to amassing collections. Dorsey provided written narratives of the collections of material gathered from the Native peoples of the Plains, Hudson the collections from California Native peoples, and Voth collections from the Hopi people. The narratives, or catalogues, were sent to major natural history museums of the day in an attempt to sell collections. The narratives appeared as typed pages, without photographs, emphasizing the level of scholarship involved in their production by referencing the ethnographers who had gathered or catalogued collections for the Harvey Company. On January 27, 1904, Dorsey wrote to Hudson: "Mr. Huckel has authorized me to engage your services to come here to Albuquerque and make a complete scientific catalogue of the big Pomo collection here." Utilizing the information that Hudson provided and capitalizing upon his reputation as an ethnographer, Huckel sent several catalogues of collections for sale to Dr. George Byron Gordon at the University Museum of Pennsylvania on November 19, 1904. They included:

Pomo basket, 9", by Alice Waris, c. 1900

> An unusually interesting collection of Hupa objects, all collected many years ago and catalogued by Dr. Hudson. . . . There are 211 specimens in the collection. Price, $1,200.00.

It is evident through the sales price associated with the Hupa collection gathered by Hudson that the profit margin on the sale of the baskets was considerable. At a cost of $1.50 each, 211 specimens would total $316. This amount, combined with Hudson's salary

Pomo feather baskets, 3", were among the objects catalogued by Dr. John Hudson for the Fred Harvey Company.

total $316. This amount, combined with Hudson's salary of approximately $150 per month, would result in a significant markup from the actual cost of the baskets.

The catalogue described the Pomo collection available for sale by the Harvey Company. Sales of this collection also reflected a considerable profit for the Indian Department:

> *A Pomo collection, believed to be the largest and most complete and certainly the most valuable ever brought together. The collection numbers about 400 specimens and has been thoroughly identified and catalogued by Dr. Hudson. Price $7000.00.*

Although the University Museum did not purchase any of the large collections, Gordon did write regarding the collections on at least two other occasions in 1906 and again in 1907 to inquire of the availability for sale.

In April 1904, after one year and four months of Fred Harvey Company employment, George Dorsey left to return to full-time work at the Field Museum. Dorsey's

OPPOSITE

Kachina doll (left), 7"-8", collected by
Frederick Volz, a trader at Canyon Diablo,
c. 1900, and (right), 9", by Charles Owen,
a curator at the Field Museum, Chicago,
c. 1911–1913

interest in working for the Fred Harvey Company appears to have been motivated at least in part by the increased monetary advantages of working within the private sector. Dorsey had initially delayed acceptance of the position of curator at the Field Museum because of the salary. In a letter dated January 1, 1904, Dorsey requested and was granted reinstatement to his full position at the Field Museum:

> *In spite of the satisfaction derived from earning a salary of very much greater magnitude than that which I received as curator for the Department of Anthropology during the past year, I have never felt the sincere satisfaction and delight which has always been mine in performing the work of the Curator of Anthropology. (Dorsey Correspondence, Field Museum of Natural History)*

After his return to full employment at the Field Museum and just two and a half months after his formal working relationship with the Indian Department ended, Dorsey requested that the Field Museum purchase 250 objects, mostly baskets, from the Fred Harvey Company for $3,410. When the purchase was not approved, Dorsey made a second request on May 8, 1905, adding a collection of 191 Wasco objects for an additional $1,200. On September 27, 1905, Dorsey requested permission to purchase Pomo and Arapaho collections for $1,816, stressing that the collections would be purchased at cost. In actuality, the Indian Department made a 300 percent profit on the sale.

CHAPTER 4

TRADERS *and* COLLECTORS

Navajo Germantown textile, 21 1/2" x 21",
c. 1900. Herman Schweizer purchased a
number of blankets and baskets from
Marietta Wetherill in 1910.

OPPOSITE
John Lorenzo Hubbell in the storeroom at Ganado in the early 1900s

*I have been looking over our Hopi pottery here, that was shipped from
Albuquerque, and it is not nearly as good as the pottery you showed me at
Ganado. The better quality sells faster with us.*
—J. F. HUCKEL TO TRADER J. L. HUBBELL, *January 10, 1905*

Huckel and Schweizer relied upon regional traders to supply the Native American–made
objects displayed and sold at the Harvey Company facilities. Suppliers included
Frederick Volz, who operated a trading post at Canyon Diablo, and Samuel Eldot, who
managed a store at San Juan Pueblo.

Many of the small items purchased for sale to tourists were acquired from Jesus Sito
Candelario, who owned and operated the Original Old Curio Store at 301-303 San
Francisco Street in Santa Fe. Initially the business was called the Original Jake Gold
Curio Store, but Candelario and Gold severed a working relationship in June 1903. The
Fred Harvey Company bought small ceramics from Candelario, initially purchasing fifty
"rain gods"—small figurative ceramics made at the pueblo of Tesuque that were popular
with tourists—in December 1903. Candelario's sales records reveal orders placed by the
Fred Harvey Company on August 29, 1904, for "100 small rain gods along with a few
of the large black ones" and on April 12, 1905, an order of "one hundred Tesuque

Anastacia Vigil makes Tesuque rain gods in the early 1900s.

pottery gods, small size and fifty of the larger size black gods." On September 2, 1904, the Harvey Company requested, "Please send us by baggage car about 200 assorted small pieces of pottery, which we can sell at retail from 15 cents to 25 cents." On May 7, 1906, the Harvey Company ordered 100 small rain gods, three dozen larger ones, and one dozen Chimayo scarfs. Pottery continued to be central to tourist sales as reflected by an order of "300 small Santa Clara pottery, equally divided in red and black from 7 1/2 to 15 cents" placed by the Harvey Company on November 7, 1906.

In 1910, Herman Schweizer purchased an extensive collection of Navajo material from Marietta Wetherill, widow of Richard Wetherill. Richard Wetherill and his brother-in-law, Charlie Mason, had discovered Cliff Palace at Mesa Verde in 1888 and subsequently displayed prehistoric pottery at the 1893 Field Columbian Exposition in Chicago. After conducting archaeological field work for the Hyde Exploring Expedition at Chaco Canyon, Richard Wetherill established a trading post near the site of Pueblo Bonito in 1897. Initially started to stock supplies for the Hyde Exploring Expedition, the trading post at Pueblo Bonito became popular with Navajo people who had previously found it necessary to ride thirty to forty miles to Farmington for supplies. The trading post continued to operate under the shadow of Pueblo Bonito until the death of Richard Wetherill on June 22, 1910. Marietta Wetherill and her five small children found themselves in financial straits after her husband's death. It was necessary for her to liquidate all her assets, including Navajo textiles and baskets. In her memoirs, Marietta Wetherill tells of Herman Schweizer's visit to Chaco Canyon to purchase items from the Wetherill collections:

> In 1911 [1910], I sold the bayetta blankets to Herman Schweizer, the buyer for the Santa Fe Railroad [Fred Harvey Indian Department]. . . . I told him I had a team of horses and a man capable of taking him to Pueblo Bonito from Gallup two days from now.

"Anything I show you is for sale", I said, "I'll price it to you and if you want it at my price you can have it . . . . I sold him a Ponca [poncho] robe with the split in the top for your head for twenty-five hundred. He was there three or four days before he gave me a second check for thirty-seven thousand dollars". (Fred Harvey Blanket Ledgers at the Heard Museum and Wetherill probate records noted in Frank McNitt's book, Richard Wetherill: Anasazi, do not reflect assets approaching the amounts stated here.)

Significant collections for both the museum and sales room were acquired from trader John Lorenzo Hubbell of Ganado. Extensive orders of textiles were acquired from Hubbell along with purchases of jewelry, pottery, and basketry. These objects were transported by wagon from the trading post at Ganado to the train depot in Gallup where they were shipped courtesy of the Santa Fe Railway to Albuquerque. Shipments, including pottery, were recorded according to weight in pounds.

Schweizer started doing business with J. L. Hubbell, just after the Indian Department opened. Their correspondence testifies to their enduring business relationship and friendship. Schweizer also made purchases for the Indian Department from Ramon and Lorenzo, Hubbell's sons, who ran trading operations away from Ganado. Dorothy Hubbell, J. L. Hubbell's daughter-in-law, remembered Schweizer's visits to Ganado and the respectful business relationship shared by the two men. Each Indian blanket in the rug room at Ganado had a coded tag listing the cost and the retail price. Dorothy Hubbell recalls that Schweizer was the only person other than family members or employees who had access to the Hubbell pricing code: "He was the only one [Hubbell] ever did that for. He was very fond of Mr. Schweizer. And he felt that he knew rugs. And he would know the worth of the value of a rug. And you had to know rugs to buy them." The Harvey Indian Department was Hubbell's largest customer.

Santa Ana jars, 15", c. 1830–1880

Zuni bowl, 18 1/2" diameter, c. 1900, collected by Frederick Volz and sold to the Harvey Company

Navajo Germantown textile, 15" x 37", c. 1900, acquired from Marietta Wetherill in 1910

OPPOSITE
The Fred Harvey Company acquired Hopi kachina dolls, 10"–12", from trader Frederick Volz, c. 1900. From left: Katsinmana, Mountain Lion Katsinas, and Hiilili

Schweizer was a tough customer. Repeatedly, he rejected half a lot of jewelry or blankets, reasoning that the quality was poor and he would not stock poor quality merchandise in Harvey establishments. His letters were critical and to the point. However, Hubbell must have taken them in stride, because this firm business relationship lasted until Hubbell's death in 1930 and then continued with his sons.

Besides quality, Schweizer directed suppliers like Hubbell as to what they should send, including size and color. In letters to Hubbell, Schweizer wrote:

We can use more of the plain swastika rings and I believe I wrote you I can use more of the snake bracelets, plain, about 3 or 4 dozen more and perhaps 200 to 300 rings. (April 24, 1906)

There were not many fine blankets in this shipment, and could use a lot of small, well made grays or grays with red from $5.00 to $12.00. (February 5, 1906)

I was compelled to return the modern rings at $2.00, as we could not make any money on them. They are too crude and are not worth any such price. I was also compelled to return to you today the 50 turquoise mounted bracelets, which we cannot use as we are getting much better stock than that for less money. (January 8, 1906)

I do not want any ordinary Mochi [Moqui or Hopi] pottery, but only the fine bowls, and do not want any of those high jars, as they do not sell. (March 13, 1907)

These terse excerpts illustrate how decisions were made on what to stock in Harvey Indian Department establishments. The business was obviously market-driven and preserving the Harvey Company quality image was preeminent. Schweizer did not decide what to buy from suppliers in an arbitrary way. If a certain product style, color, or type did not sell, Schweizer and Huckel did not want to continue to carry it or others like it in inventory. These are the same techniques embraced by corporate America in scientific inventory management.

The same business principles guided Schweizer in his Indian Department purchases; the customer actually determined what the Indian Department would carry in stock. Large, expensive, or breakable objects were not practical souvenirs for the average tourist. As tourists purchased weavings, pottery, silver, and other objects, Schweizer attempted to replace his inventory with items like the ones he had sold.

Attempts by Huckel and Schweizer to influence Native American arts they purchased is most evident in the Navajo textiles they bought through Hubbell. In 1908, the Harvey Company purchased a total of 1,657 textiles, and in 1909, 2,094 textiles. Other key individuals who supplied Navajo and Hispanic textiles to the Harvey Company include Pedro Muñoz, Julian Padilla, and Juan Olivos.

Huckel to a small extent, and Schweizer to a greater one, specified colors and materials in the Navajo textiles that were acquired from Hubbell and sold in Harvey establishments. Strongly opposing the use of cotton for the foundation fibers in Navajo rugs, Schweizer wrote in a letter to Hubbell dated September 12, 1907:

I learn that cotton warp blankets are again being made on the reservation in great quantities.

When we started in the curio business several years ago, we made it a point to keep the general public informed in regard to cotton warp blankets, and succeeded to a great extent in killing the sale of this class of goods.

When cotton string is used for warp, the blanket is not at all durable, as it breaks very easily, and as you know, when the warp in a blanket breaks, the blanket is worthless. Native wool blankets should be all wool, and I believe it is necessary that we must again keep this information before the public at all times, not only to

protect our own interests, but in an endeavor to again stop as much as possible, the production of cotton warp blankets.

Schweizer also attempted to influence the colors used by contemporary weavers as
evidenced in a letter dated July 15, 1908, to Hubbell. This letter also establishes one of
Schweizer's marketing theories:

> By the way, can't you arrange to use more of the brown wool in your blankets? People are
> getting tired of the grey body blankets with black & white designs. We have got to get up
> something new all the time to keep the public interested so they will buy. This is good
> business for you as well as us.

In a handwritten note at the end of a letter dated February 20, 1908, to Hubbell,
Schweizer wrote: "Send some more blankets 12.00 to 25.00 each but only the very fine
weaves want them with lots of red in have quite a few grays yet."

Huckel was also interested in rug colors and wrote to Schweizer about both manufactured and native dyes on March 31, 1909:

> I have several times talked with you about dyes. I bought several years ago, some dyes
> from Boston which looked as nearly like bayetta color as anything I have ever seen.
> Did you ever try this, and with what result? The dye cost quite a little,—about $10.00
> I think.
>
> I have been thinking for some time we should have our Indians use native dyes in
> some of our blankets the same as we got Mr. Voth to get the Indians to use native dyes in
> Mishognovi baskets. Some of the old Indians know how this native dye is made up, or if
> not, Dr. Pepper's and other books tell how some dyes are made.

Along with color, Schweizer also attempted to influence the designs on Navajo textiles sold through Harvey Company stores. In a letter to Hubbell dated March 4, 1908,
he comments: "And referring particularly to the swastikas these are not nearly so much
in demand as they used to be." Schweizer complains about Navajo rug designs in a letter of January 15, 1909, that "nine out of every 10 have either crosses or a double cross."

Opposite

*Navajo child's wearing blanket, 46" x 25 1/2",
purchased by the Harvey Company from Pedro
Muñoz on September 20, 1902*

J. L. HUBBELL

MAJOR SUPPLIER OF NATIVE AMERICAN ARTS and crafts to the Fred Harvey Indian Department, J. L. Hubbell also acted as recruiting agent for the Harvey Company when Native artist-demonstrators were sought to work in Harvey establishments. Between 1883 and the 1950s the Hubbell Trading Company managed thirty-two separate trading posts.

Born in Parijito, New Mexico, in 1853 to a bilingual, bicultural family, Hubbell first visited the area near what is today's Hubbell Trading Post National Historic Site in Ganado, Arizona, about 1876. In 1884 he formed a partnership with C. N. Cotton and later acquired Cotton's interest in the Ganado trading post. Hubbell acquired the Navajo name *Nákee Sinilí*, which means "eyeglasses." Hubbell was a member of the Arizona legislature and an advocate for women's right to vote, prohibition, and statehood; all became law during his lifetime.

With the success of the Ganado trading post, Hubbell established additional trading posts at Keams Canyon, Chinle, Black Mountain, Nazlini, Oraibi, Cedar Springs and Piñon Springs, and opened a store in Gallup.

J. L. Hubbell and Herman Schweizer, manager of the Fred Harvey Indian Department, had a long and enduring business relationship. On December 4, 1930, shortly after Hubbell passed away, Schweizer wrote a letter to T. E. Purdy, Atchison Topeka & Santa Fe Railway Agent in Gallup, New Mexico:

There is no doubt that Mr. Hubbell was the greatest Indian Trader, and did more in a practical way to promote the sale of their [Native American] products than anyone else. We started doing business with him about 28 years ago.

Mr. Hubbell was a man of his word, and I could always depend on him.

I might quote one incident to illustrate this.

At the time we were planning the Santa Fe Railway exhibit at San Diego for the 1915 Exposition which was called the Painted Desert, I decided that it would add to the atmosphere of the place to have a band of Navajo sheep in this village.

I had purchased old corrals at Santo Domingo, photographed them, and then placed them in the Exposition grounds in the same way that they had probably been at Santo Domingo for 50 or 100 years.

I was afraid to take up the question of sending these sheep with the Exposition officials or anyone else, as I thought perhaps somebody might object, either the health authorities or someone else might bring up an objection, although I felt if I got the sheep there everything would be all right.

I couldn't afford to have the sheep arrive at San Diego a number of days ahead of the Exposition for fear someone might raise an objection, and I could not afford to have them arrive the day after the Exposition opened. Therefore, it was necessary for the sheep to arrive at San Diego the night before the exposition opened December 31, 1914.

Therefore, the sheep had to be loaded at Gallup on a definite date, and I told Mr. Hubbell that I depended on him accordingly.

Mr. Anawalt agreed to get the sheep through on a certain fast freight so they would arrive at San Diego the evening before the Exposition opened.

I was in California at the time, about December 25th, and heard that Mr. Hubbell was sick in bed, so I was very much concerned about the sheep.

I arrived in Gallup on No. 2 in the midst of a blizzard, and was walking down the platform with my head down and bumped into somebody, and on looking I found it was Mr. Hubbell all wrapped up in a shawl and I said, "For heaven's sake, Mr. Hubbell, what are you doing here in this storm? I heard you were sick."

In his high-pitched falsetto voice, he called out: "Well you depended on me to get those sheep loaded today, and if I wasn't here you wouldn't get them. They are stuck out here about five miles in a gully, and I sent some extra men out there so as to be sure and get them in."

I don't know of any other man of my acquaintance out here who would have made good to the extent of getting up out of a sick bed to make his word good on a comparatively unimportant thing like this.

At another time I was on my way to Ganado, and met Mr. Hubbell at Saint Michael's on his way to an important political conference in Phoenix.

He insisted on going back to Ganado with me, in spite of the fact that it made no difference to him in a business way, and sent a telegram to Phoenix that he was delayed and to get along without him, otherwise to wire back and he would be able to start the next afternoon from Ganado.

The next afternoon about four o'clock a messenger came on horseback to Ganado requesting him to come to Phoenix, that they were waiting for him, and we started out in a rain storm, expecting to reach St. Michaels that night, but we couldn't make it on account of the bad roads, and both of us slept in a sheep camp that night with some Navajo boys, and it was quite thrilling to me, although Mr. Hubbell slept like a log on a sheep pelt while I kept the fire going.

Hopi jar, 12", c. 1905–1910

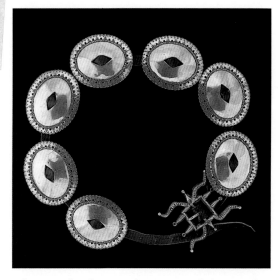

Schweizer was also influencing Navajo-made silver jewelry to be sold to tourists before the opening of the Indian Department. Through personal interviews with Schweizer, John Adair learned that Schweizer was commissioning lighter-weight jewelry as early as 1899. Silver jewelry was sold on the trains and at the stations along the routes. Schweizer initially furnished silver and turquoise stones to the trading post at Thoreau, New Mexico, where silversmiths were encouraged to produce thin, lightweight rings and bracelets. This jewelry frequently contained design elements such as arrows and "swastikas" (whirling logs) targeted for tourist purchase.

Schweizer compiled a large collection of well-made Native American jewelry which served as a guide for the lighter-weight objects sold to tourists. Although the percentage of silver content, the stamped designs, and the quality of the turquoise stones changed in the tourist jewelry, the basic concept remained the same. Native American silversmiths were encouraged to make jewelry forms such as brooches, earrings, and pendants that were not typically made and worn by southwestern Native Americans but were compatible in form to jewelry worn by Euro-Americans during the early 1900s.

Private collectors were also integral to Fred Harvey Company business activities. Many private collections that had been formed over several-year periods were purchased directly from a collector or from heirs of a deceased collector.

A collection of northern California and Plateau baskets was acquired from Miss Anne M. Lang by 1902. A Wasco basket that appears to be from the Lang collection, now at the Nelson-Atkins Museum, appeared in Otis Mason's 1904 definitive basketry book, *Aboriginal American Basketry*, published through the Bureau of American Ethnology. The Wasco basket was identified as a part of the Fred Harvey Company collection. Miss

Lang wrote from Dalles, Oregon, to the Fred Harvey Company on August 1, 1910, regarding a collection of Klickitat baskets that she had available for sale and referenced baskets she had sold in previous years:

> *Have you still the Wasco bags, called "Sally Bags," I sold you through Miss Henrietta Hamilton, of Seattle? Would it add to their value if I should send you a short sketch of Sally and the baskets vouching for their authenticity? Sally was a pensioner on our family's bounty for years and she regarded me to use her own words, "Kha - kwa miki tenas"—(like my own child). I was the innocent namer of the bags, and can trace almost every one Sally ever made. At the time I let Miss Hamilton have the bags, I intended then to lend her some proof of their authenticity, hoping to make some prints from a negative of Sally, but I was not able to do so.*
>
> *The bags you purchased are the very last Sally made.*

Another large basket collection, assembled by E. L. McLeod of California, was purchased from his sister, Miss Taylor, on June, 14, 1910, after his death. McLeod's baskets appeared prominently in Otis Mason's basketry book. A number of the McLeod baskets featured in the book remain in the Harvey Company collections at the Heard Museum and the Nelson-Atkins Museum today.

Schweizer spent much of his time on trains traveling as far east as Chicago for auctions of Indian art objects. A master of buying low and selling high, Schweizer was a shrewd and careful businessman.

In addition to buying vast collections of Native American material, the Fred Harvey Company also sold collections to museums and private collectors. Among the many private individuals who purchased from the Harvey Company, perhaps none was quite so well known as newspaper tycoon William Randolph Hearst. Hearst became interested in acquiring Harvey Company Native American arts after seeing a Harvey Company display in Chicago. He then pressed Herman Schweizer to sell collections from the display. Schweizer wrote a letter advising that the material was for advertisement of the Southwest for the Santa Fe Railway. Hearst was not so easily dissuaded. He entered into many years of purchasing with the Harvey Company, buying an extensive collection of Navajo chief blankets.

Wasco basket, 6 3/4", featured as part of the collection of the Fred Harvey Company in Otis Mason's 1904 book. This was probably one of the "Sally Bags" that the Harvey Company acquired from Miss Anne M. Lang.

OPPOSITE

Top two: Navajo silver bracelets, late 1800s; Bottom two: Navajo silver bracelets made for sale to tourists. The Fred Harvey Company purchased many snake bracelets from trader J. L. Hubbell; Right: Navajo concha belt, 44 1/2", c. 1900

Baskets collected by E. L. McCleod were illustrated in Otis Mason's 1904 book and purchased in 1910 by the Fred Harvey Company. Top left: Panamint, Kawaiisu, or Kitanemuk, 8" height, c. 1890–1900; middle: Yokuts, 30 1/2" diameter, c. 1890–1900; bottom: Kitanemuk, 19" diameter, c. 1890–1900; below: Kawaiisu, 10" height, c. 1890–1900

Hearst was not an easy customer. He demanded a discount, was slow to pay his bills, and demanded of Schweizer material that was not available for sale but set aside for the Harvey Company museum in Albuquerque. Hearst was successful at times in securing the treasured objects, frequently Navajo blankets, that he desired. Because of his power and his value as a customer, Herman Schweizer and J. F. Huckel corresponded at length about the dilemma of overdue bills by Hearst.

As owner of one of the country's major newspapers, Hearst was one of the most powerful and intimidating men in America. The Harvey organization did not wish to incur his wrath, but they needed to collect their receivables. In one letter, Hearst alludes to all the Grand Canyon publicity appearing in his newspapers. Using high pressure tactics, Hearst offered to publish a large article on the Canyon in return for an additional 5 percent discount to be added to the unauthorized 20 percent discount he had already taken. In a letter discussing Hearst's past due accounts, Ford Harvey, company president, wrote to Schweizer on March 21, 1917:

> You have been so successful in the past in handling the business with Mr. Hearst that I hesitate to offer you advice. On the other hand would like to know what you think should be done. If you could obtain the $3,418.09 which has been due us for almost two years it would be gratifying.

Hearst collected 186 textiles over more than four decades. Of these, 158 (85 percent) came through the Harvey Company.

Another private collector who purchased from the Harvey Company was basket collector Homer Sargent. Sargent was a Pasadena resident who was closely affiliated with the Field Museum in Chicago and whose private collection of baskets totaled more than 800. Sargent purchased baskets from the Harvey Company in Albuquerque as early as May 1902. Purchases from the Indian Building in Albuquerque on September 3, 1903, included a Chemehuevi basket now at the Field Museum. On June 1, 1907, he purchased at the Grand Canyon a miniature basket made by Pomo basketmaker Joseppa Dick, who demonstrated basketmaking at the Indian Building in Albuquerque in 1903.

Helen Stewart with her basket collection
in the early 1900s

After the initial flurry of activity that required the presence of both Huckel and Schweizer in Albuquerque, and after Schweizer proved his competence at purchasing and selling Indian arts and crafts products and at managing and expanding the Indian Department, Huckel spent less time in New Mexico. He turned the day-to-day operations of the Indian Department over to Schweizer. Funds for buying individual objects and entire collections were readily available. Schweizer apparently had a free hand when it came to making purchases.

One important collection did become available. Shortly before the Harvey Company's La Fonda Hotel opened in Santa Fe in 1926, Schweizer purchased the collection of Governor L. Bradford Prince. Examples of Pueblo pottery, Southwestern clothing, and Hispanic religious paintings, or santos, comprised the collection.

By the mid-1920s, it had become difficult to obtain old and rare Indian objects. In a 1927 letter, J. F. Huckel, always a hard taskmaster, admonished Schweizer to get out on the

road to purchase collections before they slipped away to other museums and collectors:

> I have been looking around in Southern California and find all kinds of Indian goods and baskets and in some instances these collections have been secured within a year. These people simply went after them or kept in touch with the source of supply. We are almost all out of them. I was quite upset about this matter at the time as I felt if you had a suitable assistant he could do some of this work for you. I wrote and congratulated you on buying the collection near Santa Fe and such a collection, while I appreciate the difficulty to purchase, this was really in our territory but we should not overlook other territory, should we, where goods could be obtained we can readily sell. There is a chance of our buying out a large collection that we could turn into money very quickly.
>
> This letter is not personal, but entirely impersonal, simply business. Let us get together on this matter. (Huckel then added a handwritten postscript:) It is more important than you realize.

Taking this admonition to heart, Schweizer went to Las Vegas, Nevada, less than six weeks after Huckel's letter and purchased 550 baskets from the Helen J. Stewart estate. The sale of the baskets was noted in the newspaper *Las Vegas Age* on March 19, 1927: "The consideration of $12,500 was paid in cash within an hour after Mr. Schweizer examined the collection. The collection, consisting of many finely woven Panamint baskets, was carefully packed and shipped to Albuquerque."

Sales of older materials to museums peaked before World War I. One of the buyers who continued to purchase during the depression years was Maie Bartlett Heard of Phoenix, Arizona. Records from 1930, one year after

LEFT
Two Chemehuevi baskets, 3"–4", c. 1900, purchased by Homer Sargent from the Fred Harvey Company in Needles, California, on January 20, 1915

Panamint basket collected by Helen Stewart, 6", c. 1900. This basket can be seen in the photograph, opposite, of Helen Stewart with her collection.

A Saltillo serape, 74" x 44", c. 1800–1850, purchased by Maie Heard from the Harvey Company in 1930

the opening of the Heard Museum, reveal purchases of Saltillo serapes, Navajo blankets, baskets, beadwork, and silver jewelry. In December 1930, Herman Schweizer wrote to Mrs. Heard about purchases of baskets from the Helen Stewart collection as well as a Saltillo serape:

> *Regarding the old zarape, I have never seen one woven as fine as this. I purchased it myself in Mexico many years ago, and it has been in our vault for twenty years with a few others which we are keeping in a collection, but I was persuaded to let you have this, as Mr. McDevitt told me you wanted a red one to go with the blue one you purchased.*
>
> *The zarape belonged to a wealthy family in the City of Mexico named Jimenez, and at the time they sold it they were trying to raise money to buy an auto. I found the zarape in a curio shop where it was on consignment, as they wanted more money than the curio shop would pay so it was there on consignment, and I made the deal personally with the owners.*
>
> *It is truly a museum specimen.*

The price of this Saltillo was $750.00, the same price Mrs. Heard had paid in earlier months for another Saltillo. After billing was received, Maie Heard wrote to the Harvey Company on April 8, 1930, requesting a discount, stating: "As I am buying for a museum, I feel that there should be some discount from your regular tourist prices. Am I not correct?" Harvey Company Indian Department employee Ed McDevitt worked with Schweizer and responded on April 24 on behalf of the Harvey Company and referenced Schweizer in his letter: "He wishes the writer to advise that it is quite customary to give discounts to museums on modern paintings. However, this consideration is not granted on the old pieces such as baskets, beadwork, blankets, and pottery."

McDevitt's correspondence reveals company policy and practice in another letter to Maie Heard on April 9, 1930:

> *We note that you feel there should be some discount in as much as you are buying for a museum. Frequently our customers make the same request, but under no circumstances are we allowed to grant a reduction, due to a policy long established by the company. At the*

present time we are as much interested in buying the genuine old pieces as selling them, and it is a fact that today we pay as much for the unusual articles as we used to sell them for five years ago. We hope you do not misunderstand our attitude as we are anxious to serve you.

One of the last Harvey Company institutional clients of major collections was the Nelson-Atkins Museum of Art, newly founded in Kansas City, Missouri, in 1933. J. F.

Huckel, a Kansas City resident, was enthusiastic about the sale of art to the Nelson-Atkins. His enthusiasm was not matched by Herman Schweizer, who had been carefully building the museum collection at the Alvarado in Albuquerque for more than thirty years. Schweizer was instructed by Huckel to select the objects for the sale. In so doing, many of the objects Schweizer selected closely resembled others that remained in the Fred Harvey museum collection in Albuquerque.

In 1935, the Albuquerque Harvey office arranged to lend Native American paintings as well as collections of Southwestern objects to the Nelson-Atkins Museum for a special exhibit. Photographs from the display reveal the inclusion of a painting by Tse Ye Mu which belonged to Mary Jane Colter. Colter decorated many of the Harvey Company hotels with paintings and maintained a private collection of her own. She later gave many paintings to avid art collector and daughter of Ford Harvey, Katherine Harvey. J. F. Huckel also formed a collection of paintings, which was given to Katherine.

LEFT

Untitled painting by Tse Ye Mu, 32" x 34", c. 1920–1930. Mary Jane Colter decorated one of the rooms at La Fonda Hotel with this painting. It was later displayed at an exhibit at the Nelson-Atkins Museum in 1935.

CHAPTER 5

CREATING *an* ATTRACTION

❖

> The unique Indian Colony in the Harvey Collection rooms is increasing rapidly . . . the
> colony workshop represents a busy scene and throngs of visitors are greatly interested in the
> manipulations of the artisans.
> —ALBUQUERQUE JOURNAL-DEMOCRAT, *February 11, 1903*

At the Fred Harvey Company Indian Building at The Alvarado Hotel, Huckel and
Schweizer placed artist-demonstrators in a room with tree branches and painted backgrounds to simulate the natural environment of Navajo weavers, who frequently wove
out of doors. Newspaper articles reported on the "colonies" of Native Americans living
at the Alvarado. The adapted world's fair formula, which offered live Native Americans,
attracted media attention that would continue for four decades. In 1903 Apache, Navajo,
Isleta, and Hopi people were hired to serve as a visible presence inside the Indian
Building and to demonstrate the craft arts that were sold. Many of the artist-demonstrators lived in a pueblo style dwelling adjacent to The Alvarado Hotel. The building
provided a colorful backdrop for tourist photography.

The public viewed a visit to exhibits at world's fairs in Chicago in 1893 and St. Louis
in 1904 as a chance to step into another world. Although narrower in scope and less elaborate, a visit to a Harvey Company Indian Department exhibit offered the public thrills

Apache basket, 19", c. 1900

OPPOSITE
*Elle of Ganado (fifth from left), Clara
Kinlicheenie (left), and her mother, Adzaa
Yahzi (next to Clara) were among the
Navajo weavers who served as artist-
demonstrators at the Indian Building at
The Alvarado Hotel in the early 1900s.*

Apache basketweavers at the Fred Harvey Indian Building in Albuquerque in 1903

similar to those experienced by today's visitors to Walt Disney's Magic Kingdom. In April 1990, author Frank Waters recalled that "The F. H. [Fred Harvey] Indian Building at the Santa Fe station was equal to any modern museum, and all transcontinental trains were stopped there for thirty minutes."

Huckel and Schweizer had difficulty finding Native American artists who were willing to leave their homes for extended periods of time to work in Albuquerque. On several occasions, one or both wrote to John Lorenzo Hubbell of Ganado enlisting his assistance in finding Native people who would be willing to live and work at the Indian Building while abiding by Harvey Company rules.

It is likely that two Navajo employees, Elle and Tom of Ganado, were brought to the attention of the Fred Harvey Company by J. L. Hubbell. Elle and Tom began working for the Fred Harvey Indian Department around 1903, continued their employment for more than twenty years, and served as the initial major attraction to the Indian Building at the Alvarado Hotel. The Fred Harvey Company used images of Elle, and to a lesser extent of Tom, to beckon the American traveling public west by train into an exotic, comfortable, and colorful region. In advertising images promoted by the Santa Fe Railway and the Fred Harvey Company, Elle weaving at her loom personified the adventure a train trip west could offer.

Elle of Ganado first came into prominence when she won a weaving competition entitling her to the right to weave a blanket to be given to President Theodore Roosevelt when his train arrived in Albuquerque on May 5, 1903. It is not precisely clear how Elle was chosen for this honor although certainly the Harvey Company played an important role in securing this commission for her. The following description appeared in a 1904 Harvey Company publication, *The Indian and Mexican Building:*

Elle is nearing fifty years, but is full of life, and was highly elated with the important task to which she had been appointed. She came from the reservation to the Fred Harvey Indian Building at Albuquerque to do the work, and was an object of veneration by the other Navajo women who were weaving blankets alongside of her.

While she knows no English, she understood fully the importance of the "Great Father" and asked permission to be present when the blanket was presented to him. Her request was granted.

The rug—woven in red, white, and blue—served as Roosevelt's honorary membership card to the Commercial Club of Albuquerque. The newspaper accounts covering Elle and the Roosevelt rug represented some of the earliest publicity the Harvey Company received. Six national newspapers including the *Denver Post*, the *Chicago Inter-Ocean*, and the *St. Louis Globe-Democrat* carried the story. Although photographs were not prevalent in newspapers in the early 1900s, a photograph of Elle and Tom and the completed presidential blanket appeared twice in the *Albuquerque Journal-Democrat*.

Other artist-demonstrators appeared at the Indian Building in Albuquerque. Noted ethnographer Dr. John Hudson functioned as a liaison with Pomo people who came from California to serve as artist-demonstrators. In February 1903, Hudson arranged for Joseppa and Jeff Dick and Clara and Tom Mitchell to demonstrate basketweaving along with techniques of making other cultural crafts. On February 6, 1903, Hudson noted in a letter to his wife: "All the Harvey's want is the attraction to visitors and monopoly of all work done."

Musical bow, 28 1/2", and feather pendant, 12", made by William Benson. The bow was made at the Indian Building in 1904.

ELLE *of* GANADO

ELLE OF GANADO worked for the Fred Harvey Company for over twenty years. At The Alvarado Hotel in Albuquerque, Hopi House at the Grand Canyon, the Panama-Pacific International Exposition in San Francisco, and Land Shows in Chicago, Elle demonstrated Navajo weaving and represented the Fred Harvey Company and the Santa Fe Railway. Photogenic and always available to pose, Elle's image appears in more Harvey publications than any other individual associated with the Harvey Company.

Described by the Harvey Company as its "best weaver," Elle, born to the Black Sheep Clan, was known as *Asdzáá Łichíí'* (Red Woman) to Navajo people. Navajo sources believe Elle may have gone on the Long Walk and spent time in captivity at Bosque Redondo before she became associated with the Harvey Company. Her father was reported to have been of Euro-American or Mexican descent.

Industrious and hard working, she sat for more than twenty years at her blanket loom in the Indian Building next to The Alvarado Hotel where thousands of tourists watched her card and spin wool and weave Navajo blankets. Elle made natural dyes for her weavings from berries, roots, and other plants she gathered on the reservation. Her designs were often woven in black, white, gray, brown, and red woolen yarns.

Elle and her husband Tom were frequently seen in the Indian Building at the Alvarado, always available to be photographed and interpret Navajo culture. Elle of Ganado passed away in the late Fall of 1923 or early Winter of 1924, but her warmth and charm live on in dozens of photographs and publications still in circulation today.

Elle of Ganado sits next to a partially woven rug for President Theodore Roosevelt, 1903.

TOM *of* GANADO

LIKE HIS WIFE ELLE, Tom of Ganado, known as *Naaltsoos Neiyéhé* ("Mail Carrier") worked for the Harvey Company for many years. Both were photographed by Karl Moon and their images were used to promote tourism in the Southwest.

Tom was born to the Many Goats clan. Elle's parents initially rejected him as a suitor for their daughter because he already had seven wives. However, Tom was tenacious and even though he had neither sheep nor ponies to offer for Elle's hand in marriage, the November 1922 issue of *Illustrated World* notes, "One fine June morning, only the tracks of his favorite pony were left as payment for his stolen bride."

Tom and Elle had no children of their own; however, they cared for several of Tom's grandchildren from his other marriages. These children appear with Tom and Elle in many photographs taken during that time.

Tom carried the mail between Gallup and Hubbell's Trading Post at Ganado for some time, which accounts for his being known as "Mail Carrier." He travelled with Elle to San Francisco, the Grand Canyon, and Chicago and acted as host and interpreter of language and culture. He also translated for Elle, who only spoke Navajo. Tom was fluent in the English, Spanish, Navajo, and Hopi languages.

Tom was well known in Albuquerque and was often mentioned by name in local papers. His struggle with pneumonia commanded attention in the October 3, 1904 issue of the *Albuquerque Morning Journal*. He again was the subject of a large article in the same publication on October 21, 1904. The latter account tells of the healing ceremony performed by Miguelito, a Navajo medicine man. Tom was not cured of pneumonia by the doctors at St. Joseph's Hospital in Albuquerque, so Miguelito was called upon to apply his healing skills. Evidently he had more success than the doctors, because Tom went on to lead a productive life until the late 1920s.

Tom and Elle of Ganado (center back) inside the Indian Building in the early 1900s

Pomo basketweavers William and Mary Benson, late 1800s. The Bensons wove baskets and made other cultural crafts at the Indian Building in Albuquerque in 1904 on their way to the Louisiana Purchase Exposition in St. Louis.

The Harvey Company encouraged news coverage for the artist-demonstrators in the *Albuquerque Morning Journal.* Joseppa Dick was specifically mentioned in the articles for the miniature baskets she wove, some of which were the size of a pea. Records show that the Harvey Company sold baskets woven by Joseppa, but none of her baskets have been identified in the Harvey Company collections to date.

In 1904 Hudson again arranged for Pomo people to serve as artist-demonstrators at the Indian Building. Basketweavers William and Mary Benson were in Albuquerque demonstrating the making of baskets and other cultural crafts before traveling to the Louisiana Purchase Exposition in St. Louis. While at the Indian Building, William Benson made a musical bow which was admired by Stewart Culin of the Brooklyn Museum. Several baskets in the Harvey Company collection at the Heard Museum appear to be the work of Mary Benson while the musical bow, a bone dagger, and a feather pendant are the work of William Benson.

The Fred Harvey Company, working with funds from the Santa Fe Railway, successfully created attractions in cities other than Albuquerque. In 1904 Arthur Seligman, a prominent figure in New Mexico Territory and treasurer of the New Mexico board of managers of the Louisiana Purchase Exposition, asked the Harvey Company to develop an exhibit that would represent New Mexico. This was the first major exposition the Harvey Company developed for the Santa Fe Railway. Many other more elaborate endeavors would occur in future years. Preparations for the exhibit once again received coverage in local newspapers with the following appearing in the *Albuquerque Morning Journal* of May 19, 1904:

> *The ethnological exhibit to be installed . . . will be the most extensive ever made at this or any other fair. It will be installed under the direction of Mr. J. F. Huckel, who is now in Albuquerque, and Professor George A. Dorsey.*

The exhibit was displayed in room 111 of the Anthropology Building at the World's Fair in St. Louis and was described by Huckel to the *Albuquerque Morning Journal* on May 20, 1904, as "an entirely scientific display." The Harvey Company won four awards at

the exposition including "The grand prize for the best ethnological exhibit, two gold medals, and the grand prize for the Navajo blanket exhibit." The *Albuquerque Morning Journal* ecstatically reported the results on November 5, 1904, noting that the Fred Harvey Company exhibit surpassed the exhibit of the Smithsonian Institution:

Certificate of award from Louisiana Purchase Exposition held in St. Louis in 1904

A report just received from the World's fair in St. Louis states that the Fred Harvey Indian exhibits in the division of anthropology have been awarded four prizes. The Grand Prize for the best ethnological exhibit, two gold medals, and the grand prize for the Navajo blanket exhibit. . . . The winning of the two grand prizes is worthy of note, for in both the ethnological and blanket exhibits the Harvey collections were pitted against those of the Smithsonian Institute, heretofore believed to be the finest in existence.

One of the exposition judges was George Dorsey. Well known in anthropological circles, Dorsey was a logical choice to serve as juror. It is not known whether Dorsey actually participated in the Harvey Company installation or the company simply employed his name to once again emphasize the scientific nature of the collection.

After the Louisiana Purchase Exposition in 1904, the Harvey Company continued to employ artist-demonstrators to attract tourists. Throughout the early years of the Indian Department, Elle of Ganado served as an important drawing card for the Indian Building at the Alvarado. Between the years 1909 and 1913, Elle wove another rug for another president, William

Pomo basket by Mary Benson, 35" diameter, c. 1900

5727. Navajo Indian Blanket Weaver

Copr. H. H. Tammen Co.

This postcard shows Elle of Ganado
with the rug she wove for President Taft.

Howard Taft, once again at the Harvey Company's request. As before, reference to a "presidential rug" was used in Harvey Company promotional literature. A small, twenty-page, highly illustrated brochure produced by the Fred Harvey Company includes a photograph of Elle with the rug woven for Taft. The caption reads:

> *Elle of Ganado, most famous of all the blanket weavers among the Navaho Indians, has been weaving blankets at the Indian Building in Albuquerque for many years. It was she who made the blanket presented to President Roosevelt by the Rough Riders of New Mexico. This picture shows her at work on the blanket that was presented to President Taft.*

The Harvey Company used the image of Elle of Ganado extensively in publications firmly establishing her as an icon. Elle was promoted by the Harvey Company as the weaver of the presidential rugs, and the best Navajo weaver. Elle had the distinction along with the Hopi-Tewa potter Nampeyo of being identified by name in early publications produced by the Fred Harvey Company while hundreds of other Native Americans remained anonymous. Even in records kept by the Harvey Company and Indian traders, many weavers were identified by affiliation with their husbands. In the detailed blanket ledgers maintained by the Indian Department, weavers are often referred to by the names of their husbands such as "Joe's wife" for the wife of Joe Tippicanoe, another Indian Department employee, or "Silversmith's wife." Generally, the names mentioned in the ledgers referred to John Lorenzo Hubbell, other traders, and collectors from whom the textiles were purchased rather than the weavers. Weavings purchased from "Elle" are listed as such.

In addition to serving as a primary artist-demonstrator who received notoriety and her own publicity, Elle of Ganado became a cover girl for the Harvey Company and the Santa Fe Railway. She was photographed in front of the Indian Building sign at the Alvarado with guest celebrities that included actress Mary Pickford and actor Douglas Fairbanks.

Hopi poncho, 36", late 1800s, displayed
at the Louisiana Purchase Exposition and
later sold to the American Museum of
Natural History

Navajo child's wearing blanket, 47" x 31 1/2",
c. 1875, from the J. F. Huckel collection

Elle of Ganado appeared with Mary Pickford on the cover of the March 1917 issue of The Santa Fe Magazine.

Elle escaped a photographic session with dog star Rin Tin Tin and the entire baseball team of the Chicago Cubs, although husband Tom can be seen in the photographs. Photographs of Elle and Tom with celebrities were used in different Harvey Company publications and in *The Santa Fe Magazine* which in the early 1900s served as an employee newsletter. The photograph of Elle with Mary Pickford was used on the March 1917 cover of *The Santa Fe Magazine*.

References to Elle and her accomplishments were featured in publications by other authors including George Wharton James' *Indian Blankets and Their Makers*:

> *Elle of Ganado . . . has been steadily engaged at weaving by Fred Harvey for over a dozen years. Scores of thousands have seen her, seated at the loom, in the Fred Harvey Indian rooms at Albuquerque, New Mexico, at various fairs, and in the Land Shows and other exhibits in Chicago.*

Elle also had a cameo role in the 1912 film *The Tourists* starring Mabel Normand. In this film, Elle can briefly be seen carding wool. Her facial expression conveys her amusement toward the antics in the film. Normand stars as Trixie, a caricature of Euro-American women, who travels to Santa Clara Pueblo.

Elle was a primary attraction for the Indian Department not only at the Alvarado Hotel but also in other parts of the United States. Elle and Tom were sent to the Grand Canyon at the opening of Hopi House in 1905 to demonstrate weaving. The Indian Department benefitted from the willingness of Elle and Tom to travel and live at places like the Grand Canyon. Many native peoples found it extremely difficult to live away from community and family obligations for extended periods of time, but Elle and Tom did not have obligating family ties. Although Elle was often pictured in publications and postcards with two young girls and a little boy, Tom's grandchildren, she had no children of her own. Bajhe and Tulle were the names of the girls. The boy, Paul Willie, lived with Elle and Tom during World War I in the pueblo-style building adjacent to the Alvarado.

Although Elle and Tom returned home to Ganado, Arizona, for several months at a time, they were willing to work at different Harvey Company facilities for extensive

periods. Both Elle and Tom were viewed as valuable resources by Schweizer.

By 1905, the Indian Department had become increasingly dependent upon Elle and Tom to be present at different Harvey Company establishments. While Elle served as an attraction for tourists through weaving textiles, Tom acted as a host or greeter to visitors at the Indian Building and facilitated sales of the craft arts sold there. Fluent in four languages, Tom was an asset to the Harvey Company as he could easily converse with English-speaking tourists, with Spanish-speaking people, and with the Hopi and Navajo artist-demonstrators. A newspaper report discussed Tom's working relationship with visitors to the Indian Department in the following manner:

Elle of Ganado with Paul Willie, early 1900s

> Tom has been with the Harvey system here for nearly two years, and in that time has become one of the most useful men about the big establishment. He is not merely a picturesque ornament. He works, knows the details of the business thoroughly and but for his frankness in dealing with customers, would make an excellent salesman. Tom, however, sticks rigidly to the truth and has no hesitancy in speaking his convictions accordingly when a prospective purchaser comes to the curio department. Tom's opinion of the individual is quietly formed and as quickly announced. Numerous amusing incidents are told of

Tom of Ganado was photographed frequently in front of the Indian Building. He is seen here with the Chicago Cubs, c. 1920s.

OPPOSITE
Hopi kachina dolls, 11"–12", were displayed at the Louisiana Purchase Exposition and later sold to the American Museum of Natural History. From left: Nuvaktsina, Sivu'ikwiwtaqa, Angak'tsina, and Katsinmana.

his estimates of tourists and others who come onto the place. And usually they are right. (Albuquerque Morning Journal, October 3, 1904)

On several occasions, Elle and Tom traveled on behalf of the Indian Department to other locations. In 1909 the Harvey Company sent Elle, along with anonymous southwestern artists, to a land and cattle show in Chicago that promoted travel to the Southwest. The Harvey Company utilized Santa Fe Railway funds to erect Southwestern-style buildings at the Coliseum in Chicago for these events. Southwestern craft arts were displayed and Elle and others demonstrated the creation of craft arts. The artist-demonstrators drew such a crowd that they were escorted by policemen when seeing the sights of Chicago. In 1910 Elle and Tom returned to another land and cattle show and were accompanied by the renowned Hopi-Tewa potter Nampeyo. Newspaper coverage stated:

> *Tom and Elle of Ganado, the Navajo silversmith and blanket weaver of the local Harvey curio shop with their children, will accompany the Hopi delegation to Chicago where Tom and Elle made the big hit last year. (Albuquerque Morning Journal, November 16, 1910)*

The Harvey Company received news coverage about the event in the Albuquerque newspapers:

> NAM-PE-YO AND HER FELLOW HOPIS ARRIVE HERE
> *Nam-pe-yo, the matchless pottery maker of the Hopis, and nine more of the picturesque Indians from the far-away pueblos of Walpi and Mishnongmovi, in northern Arizona, arrived in the city last night on train No. 8 from Winslow and after refreshments here, proceeded on their way to the great city of the palefaces on the shores of Lake Michigan to advertise the Santa Fe route at the Chicago Land and Irrigation exposition. . . .*

Douglas Fairbanks and Elle of Ganado (center back) at the Alvarado Indian Building in Albuquerque, c. 1920s

RIGHT
Jackie Coogan as he appeared dressed in Navajo-style clothing in 1924

These interesting Indians will afford the visitors at the land show a chance to see real Hopis at work at their crafts in the Santa Fe exhibit, dressed in native costume with surroundings made as nearly as possible to counterfeit those amid which the Hopis live when at home. (Albuquerque Morning Journal, *November 16, 1910*)

Although many Native artists traveled to the Land Show in Chicago on behalf of the Fred Harvey Company, only Elle and Tom of Ganado and Nampeyo had gained regional, if not national, recognition as reflected in the newspaper coverage that documented their travels.

The Harvey Company never failed to photograph a movie star at the Alvarado. On August 4, 1924, child movie star Jackie Coogan spent seven hours in Albuquerque. His stop there was part of a rail tour of the nation helping to promote a relief program for disadvantaged children in the Middle East. On August 8, 1924, *The Albuquerque Tribune* reported that "The idea of having the child star initiated into the Navajo tribe during his Albuquerque visit was conceived by Herman Schweizer, Superintendent of the Fred Harvey News Department at the Alvarado." Surrounded by a throng of 5,000 admirers, Coogan arrived dressed in a Navajo costume. Hoskay Yazzie, 106 years old, and other Navajo medicine men sat in a semicircle outside the Indian room awaiting the arrival of the young star. The crowd of thousands watched as Coogan became *Benay Yulthie* (Talking Eyes) in the ensuing ceremony. A photograph of Coogan appeared on the front page of the *Albuquerque Morning Journal*, August 8, 1924. After the ceremonies, Coogan stepped back on the train and continued on to other locations. Coogan, the Fred Harvey Company, and the Santa Fe Railway benefitted from the elaborate publicity generated by this event.

COMPETING EXPOSITIONS: SAN DIEGO AND SAN FRANCISCO IN 1915

A total of more than 100 million people attended the series of world's fairs held in the United States between 1876 and 1915. Always a mix of entertainment and education, they invariably featured anthropological displays of live non-European individuals.

In 1915, two Pacific coast cities competed for world's fair site selection. The opening of the Panama Canal greatly shortened the trip from the East to the Pacific coast, which had once required sailing around the tip of South America. San Diego vied with San Francisco for the honor of hosting the fair. San Diego was the first landfall on the West Coast; however, San Francisco with its larger population, money, and status, captured the right to be a host city to the fair. San Diego, not to be outdone, floated bonds, and raised the money to sponsor a smaller fair. The Santa Fe Railway financed large displays at the Panama-California Exposition in San Diego and at the Panama-Pacific International Exposition in San Francisco, developing each with equivalent sums of money. The two fairs offered a supreme opportunity for the Railway and the Fred Harvey Company to advertise a trip through the Southwest. The Santa Fe Railway took this opportunity to advertise "Two fairs for one fare" in national magazines.

Certificate of Award from the 1915 Panama-Pacific International Exposition in San Francisco

LEFT

The Santa Fe Railway funded exhibits at each 1915 exposition and offered reduced rates for passengers traveling to both. This advertisement appeared in the July 1915 issue of Good Housekeeping.

The Fred Harvey Company sent their
star weaver, Elle of Ganado, to the Panama-
Pacific International Exposition in San
Francisco in 1915.

OPPOSITE
*Dancers performed daily at the 1915 Painted
Desert Exposition in San Diego.*

In San Francisco, "The Grand Canyon of Arizona" exhibit covered five acres. It contained an Indian village, an exhibit building, and the Grand Canyon Panorama. A photograph of the exhibit building in *The Santa Fe Magazine*, July 1915, shows an Alvarado-like structure with sweeping arches. The front of the building bears a Hubbell cross. Behind the walls, traces of cacti, cliff dwellings and adobe walls peek out. Visitors to the panorama boarded a motorized coach that moved on a special track within the exhibit. It was a first-rate amusement ride within the exposition:

> *A deluxe coach . . . will accommodate thirty-five to forty passengers and will differ from an ordinary coach only in that an outlook may be had from one side only. The cars will stop at seven different stations, which were chosen because they come as nearly as possible to embracing all the differing aspects the cañon presents. The railroad reaches the cañon at "Bright Angel Trail." "Desert View," on the edge of the "Painted Desert," will reproduce exactly its desert namesake, a perfect riot of vivid colors, blue, red, yellow and green predominating, unbelievably gorgeous to one who never has seen the original, as though in some miraculous way a sunset had been carpeting the area.* (The Santa Fe Magazine, July 1914)

Herman Schweizer arranged for Elle and Tom of Ganado to work and demonstrate their crafts inside the exhibit. One photograph shows them at work in front of a mural depicting the walls of the Grand Canyon: Elle weaves at her loom while Tom stands ready to field questions and interpret Indian culture to those who flocked to this exhibit. Elle and Tom are surrounded by other Navajo adults and children. Signs describe "A Typical Indian: Navajo Winter" and the Santa Fe logo is prominently displayed. A sign placed by Elle's loom read: "Elle of Ganado, Arizona, the noted Navajo Indian weaver who uses this loom has woven special blankets for President Taft and Ex-President Roosevelt."

MARIA MARTINEZ

Louisiana Purchase Exposition where the newly wedded Maria and Julian demonstrated potterymaking techniques and where the Harvey Company won four awards for the display of blankets and baskets.

By 1915 the Martinez' were employed by the Harvey Company at the Panama-California Exposition in San Diego. Not well known to the general public in 1915, the couple lived and worked in San Diego for several months making polychrome pottery that was customary for San Ildefonso potters at that time. Two such pots remain in the Heard Museum collection today.

Maria and Julian Martinez continued a working association with the Fred Harvey Company. During the years that the Harvey Company took organized groups on "Indian Detours" into the pueblo villages near Santa Fe, Maria and Julian Martinez opened their homes to the tourists.

TWO OF THE BEST-KNOWN POTTERS of the Southwest, Maria Martinez and her husband Julian developed the black matte paint on highly polished black pottery that brought attention to the village of San Ildefonso Pueblo and changed the path of many southwestern potters. Before this pottery style was developed, Maria and Julian worked for the Fred Harvey Company. It is possible that the couple came to the attention of Harvey managers Herman Schweizer and J. F. Huckel at the 1904

LEFT
This photograph of Maria Martinez, taken around 1905, was used in a travelogue produced by the Santa Fe Railway.

Jar made by Maria and Julian Martinez, 10", c. 1915

Laura Ingalls Wilder shared her impressions of the 1915 Indian exhibit in San Francisco:

> *We went to the Indian Village, regular cliff dwellings. It is built to be a rocky cliff and one climbs up by steps cut in the solid rock all along the way. After you get up the cliff, there are holes dug into the rock, smaller, or larger where the Indians live, making baskets and pottery and weaving rugs. . . . The Indians are very friendly and good natured. (Roger Lea MacBride, West From Home, 1965)*

Other exhibitors in San Francisco built elaborate displays as well. The Union Pacific Railroad displayed a likeness of the Old Faithful Inn at Yellowstone, and the Great Northern Railroad reproduced Glacier National Park. One could also be conveyed, via a mobile platform capable of carrying 1,200 people, around a working model of the Panama Canal.

Maria Martinez (center) in San Diego in 1915, at the Painted Desert Exposition where she lived for several months. At that time, she had not received the acclaim that would be hers in later years.

San Diego, with its warm breezes and long days of sunshine, lent itself to an outdoor exhibit. The Harvey Company erected a complex, pueblo-style village on a seven-acre area of land and housed it with Native people from different cultures. At a cost of $250,000 to the Santa Fe Railway, these buildings were constructed by Native builders.

Harvey architect Mary Jane Colter, J. F. Huckel, and Herman Schweizer collaborated on ideas for the exhibit. Colter made a plaster model of the proposed design from an outline and preliminary Schweizer plan. A 1915 exhibit brochure, *Painted Desert Exposition: San Diego Exposition*, describes its historical background:

> *Realizing that many people have neither the time nor the means to visit the Indian tribes which inhabit the country adjacent to the railway from the Colorado-New Mexico line to*

OPPOSITE

Mary Pickford with Southwestern Native people at the 1915 Painted Desert Exposition in San Diego

the Pacific, and knowing the deep interest that all take in the "First Americans" it was decided to reproduce at the Panama-California Exposition at San Diego, in their Painted Desert Exhibit, typical Indian settlements of the sedentary and nomadic tribes of the Great Southwest.

A photograph of Herman Schweizer appeared on the front page of *The San Diego Union*, March 24, 1914. He and Jesse Nusbaum, noted archaeologist and construction superintendent of the Painted Desert exhibit, displayed Colter's plaster model.

The intent was to combine scientific, scenic, and artistic points of view. "The exhibit combines, to the highest degree, education, realism, ethnological truth and attractiveness of presentation." No expense was spared. Carloads of cedar fences, household articles and building materials were purchased from Native Americans and used for the pueblos, one resembling Taos and the other Zuni. Schweizer, with the help of his old friend J. L. Hubbell, smuggled a carload of sheep from Gallup to San Diego the night before the fair opened, avoiding the animal inspection authorities.

Positioned strategically on the "Isthmus," or midway section of the Panama Pacific Exposition, The Painted Desert exhibit offered a huge attraction. Newsreel footage from 1915 captured the image of President Ripley of the Santa Fe Railway during his visit to the exhibit. He can be seen amidst a spacious pueblo-style plaza being entertained by Indian dancers.

No artists, including one of the future matriarchs of pueblo pottery, Maria Martinez, were mentioned by name in any of the publicity promoting the event. Schweizer hired Maria to travel to San Diego to make chimney pots for the pueblos and her husband, Julian, to work on the construction of the pueblos. Maria, Julian, and Maria's sister, Ramoncita, worked there for the entire year of the fair.

Both the Santa Fe Railway and the Fred Harvey Company benefitted from participation in the two expositions. The Santa Fe received extensive publicity by offering passengers a reduced-fare package. The Harvey Company operated sales shops at each fair. William Randolph Hearst was but one of the customers, ordering three Navajo chief blankets from the exposition in San Diego to be delivered after the fair closed.

CHAPTER 6

PROMOTING *the* SOUTHWEST

Picturesque Names for Hotels and Trains

In view of the fact that The Trinidad Hotel already had been christened Cardeñas, the name El Tovar seemed to the best one left for the hotel at the canyon.

—WILLIAM H. SIMPSON TO FORD HARVEY, *November 6, 1920*

While The Alvarado Hotel in Albuquerque and El Tovar at the Grand Canyon were to become and remain the most famous of the many Harvey locations, lesser-known Harvey hotels in other locations were given colorful and romantic sounding regional names as well. Harvey locations with only dining rooms or lunch rooms did not receive this special designation. In a letter written to J. F. Huckel in 1929, William Haskell Simpson, the Santa Fe's general advertising agent, explains. "As the new station at Newton does not provide guest rooms, there does not seem to be any need for a special name, such as is given at other places where hotel accommodations are provided" (October 21).

This postcard of The Alvarado Hotel makes the hotel appear more expansive than it actually was.

OPPOSITE
La Fonda Hotel was purchased by the Fred Harvey Company in 1926 and redecorated by Mary Jane Colter.

Santa Fe Railway train over
Canyon Diablo

William H. Simpson's business letters reveal a quest for authentic regional names with historic meaning for hotels and railroad cars. In 1927, Simpson wrote to Charles Lummis and Herman Schweizer asking for appropriate names for railroad passenger cars for the Santa Fe's special train, "The Chief." Simpson's and the Santa Fe's success in creating colorful names for railroad cars is recounted by Lawrence Clark Powell's words as he reflects his feelings about watching trains fly by the platform in Gallup:

> *First came the westbound Chief, followed by the Grand Canyon, two sections of the California Limited, El Capitan and then the Super Chief, all running closely together, stopping only long enough to water the diesels, and finally to allow an eastbound freight to clear the yards and gather speed toward the divide.*
>
> *I am not one of those who bemoans the passing of the steam locomotive. Santa Fe's diesel fleet—its passenger engines painted red and yellow, its freight engines blue and yellow—pleases me by its trim and powerful beauty. Standing there on the platform I recited the litany of Pullman car names as they passed: Coconino Princess, Pinos Altos, Mimbres Gap, Blue Mesa, Eagle Nest, Red River Valley—and a lone New York Central car, crow among swans. . . .*
> —LAWRENCE CLARK POWELL, Books West Southwest: Essays on Writers, Their Books and Their Land, 1957

In addition to the Alvarado and El Tovar, other Harvey hotels drew rail travelers to comfortable accommodations and fine cuisine. Physical remnants of times past can be visited today in three Harvey Hotel buildings: two in Las Vegas, New Mexico, and one in Winslow, Arizona. The Montezuma, the Casteñeda, and La Posada bear mute witness to an elegant bygone era.

WILLIAM HASKELL SIMPSON

WILLIAM HASKELL SIMPSON worked for the Santa Fe Railway for nearly fifty-two years. Born on January 19, 1858, in Lawrence, Kansas, he graduated from the University of Kansas in 1880. On July 1, 1881, Simpson accepted a position as advertising clerk in the general passenger department of the Santa Fe Railroad in Topeka, Kansas. Simpson was involved with many exciting events as the Santa Fe built its tracks westward toward California. He was involved with the race with the Denver and Rio Grande Railway to conquer the route through Raton Pass, securing control for the Santa Fe Railway of the best route through Colorado into Northern New Mexico.

He transferred to the Chicago office in 1895. He was appointed general advertising agent in July 1900. This appointment proved to be one of the most visionary and profitable decisions that the management of the Santa Fe Railway would make. When the spur line from Williams to the Grand Canyon opened in 1901, Simpson sent artists on month-long excursions to the edge of the great abyss to capture its awesome grandeur on canvas. These visits by artists produced many famous paintings, drawings, and lithographs for books, postcards, and travel brochures, all glorifying the majesty of a trip west on the Santa Fe with fine food and lodging provided by the Fred Harvey Company. Many of the original paintings Simpson commissioned are now in the Santa Fe Railway corporate art collection in Schaumburg, Illinois.

On October 1918, Simpson was promoted to the position of assistant general passenger agent. During the First World War period of federal control of the railroads, he was chairman of the Western Lines' Advertising Committee and the United States Railroad Administration.

In the June 13, 1933 issue of *The Santa Fe New Mexican*, an excerpt from his obituary sums up the substance of his long and productive career:

> As an advertising expert and executive, he was in charge of what has been for all these years probably the most elaborate, ambitious and effective program of development publicity ever inaugurated by any railroad. The Santa Fe Company has led the field in the style and character of its printed business propaganda, selling Santa Fe service, and the middle west and southwest territory, its resources and opportunities, to the world.

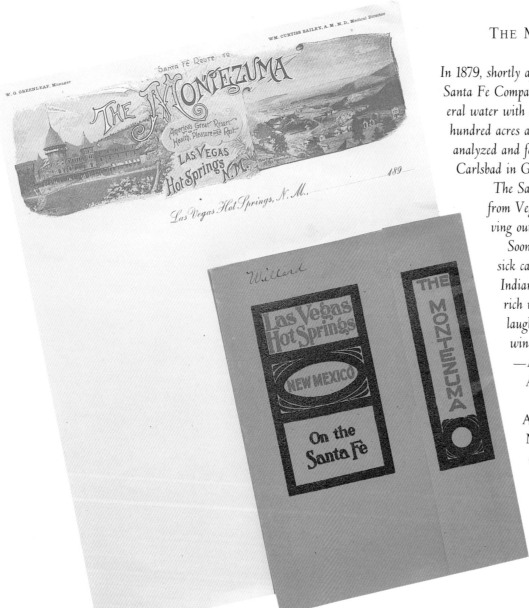

THE MONTEZUMA: LAS VEGAS, NEW MEXICO

In 1879, shortly after the coming of the railroad, the Santa Fe Company bought Hot Springs and mixed mineral water with dollars. The property consisted of eight hundred acres and thirty-two springs. The waters were analyzed and found comparable in curative powers with Carlsbad in Germany.

The Santa Fe Railroad built a branch line from Vegas, but many of the elite preferred driving out in carriages and livery hacks.

Soon millionaires, sportsmen and wealthy sick came from all parts of the world to the Indian place of magic waters. Perfume of the rich mingled with the scent of pine. Tinkle of laughter and silver drowned the whispering wind and murmuring Rio Gallinas.

—ANN NOLAN CLARK, New Mexico, August 1935

A huge and imposing edifice, the Montezuma was staffed with three hundred servants. The elegant hotel opened to the public on April 17, 1882. It was larger, more luxurious and more up-to-date than any building of its kind in New Mexico. Five special trains brought guests from many places in the world. An early 48-page brochure published by the Santa Fe Route Passenger Department advertised the spa as a place for "tourists, tired people, invalids of all classes, and those who seek a Summer or Winter Resort with the benefit to be derived from medicinal baths and mineral waters."

When the Montezuma opened, Fred Harvey was in charge of food and lodging arrangements. He would allow no canned vegetables to be served. Fresh fruit, green vegetables, shellfish and other tasty delicacies were shipped north from Guaymas and Hermosillo, Mexico. Members of the Yaqui tribe supplied the hotel with green turtles and sea celery. The 200-pound turtles were kept in a pool near the hotel. Green turtle soup and turtle steaks appeared on the Harvey menu, accompanied by sea celery used as a spicy weed to make a delicious salad.

In 1884, the Montezuma burned. Losses were covered by insurance and a new hotel was built near the site of the old one. Designed by the Chicago firm of Burnham and Root, the second Montezuma Hotel was made as fireproof as possible and a fire alarm system installed in every room. Approximately $300,000 was spent to reconstruct and refurbish this second hotel. It featured expansive balconies overlooking parks, a zoo, and Gallinas Canyon. Despite all these precautions, on August 9, 1885, The Montezuma Hotel once again burned. Undaunted by two previous disasters, The Santa Fe Railway rebuilt the hotel and appropriately re-named it the Phoenix, since it had risen from the ashes of a former hotel, but the name did not catch on, and the hotel continued to be known as the Montezuma. This third edifice contained 81,600 square feet and stood four stories tall. In spite of the grand effort put forth by the Santa Fe Railway, the Montezuma, with its beautiful setting against the mountains of the Pecos wilderness area, its elegant Queen Anne architecture and its luxurious furniture and decorations, was not a success. During this time the railroad built other hotels farther west, a bank crisis took place in the United States, and a railroad strike occurred.

The Montezuma Hotel was used as a set for the 1977 motion picture *The Evil* starring Richard Crenna. In much need of repair, the Montezuma sits today above the Armand Hammer World College campus.

Stationery and booklet from The Montezuma Hotel

THE CASTEÑEDA: LAS VEGAS, NEW MEXICO

Opened in 1898, The Casteñeda Hotel, situated adjacent to the Santa Fe Depot, has a dining room, large ballroom, and about forty guest rooms upstairs housed in its 25,000 square feet:

> *A magnificent flight of stairs, in solid oak, gives access from the office at the upper floor. The bar and billiard room is a bijou, defying description. Octagonal settee in oak and leather, agee cypress bar across the corner, sideboard of glass and cypress, cut glass Flemish tankards, hand painted china, handsome jardinieres, oxidized brass chairs and small tables—in a word, a place where one can sit for hours to enjoy the beauty of surroundings.*
> —Michelle Llamas, The New Mexican, 1974

Postcard of The Casteñeda Hotel

H-1054 HOTEL CASTANEDA, LAS VEGAS, NEW MEXICO. (C) Fred Harvey.

> *Of the furniture it may be said that the Harvey Eating-house Systems expended $30,000 . . . the bar and billiard room is a bijou, defying description. . . .*
>
> *On the sleeping floor carpets of Axminster velvet cover the halls, grill work and silk tapestries close apertures, rooms are covered in Wilton or spread with Turkish rugs, while the furniture in mahogany and maple consists for each room of wardrobe, dresser, washstand, writing desk, lounging chair, rocker, decorated crockery, imported bedstead of brass and black enamel, box springs and 40-pound hair mattress. The rooms, each with walls painted in different color or tint are large, light and well ventilated.*
> —Louis Harris Ivers, Native American Art, 1974

As with all Harvey hotels, guests were made to feel they were staying in the most comfortable accommodations in that particular location because of the Harvey reputation for great comfort and service.

Like the Montezuma, the Casteñeda was used as a movie set. In 1983, *Red Dawn*, starring Patrick Swayze, was filmed at the hotel.

MIGUELITO

MIGUELITO WAS A NAVAJO CHANTER of great power. He was born while the Navajo people were at Bosque Redondo about 1865, to the Place-Where-He-Comes-Out clan. He came to Ganado and married Maria Antonio, who later was an artist-demonstrator for the Harvey Company in Albuquerque. He lived south of Hubbell's Trading Post at Ganado near a geologic feature called Red Point. Later in his life, Miguelito was known as Red Point.

Miguelito worked for the Fred Harvey Company for long periods of time. In 1915 and 1916, he traveled to San Francisco and San Diego where he worked at Harvey Company exhibits at these two world's fairs.

Miguelito assisted with the selection and creation of sandpainting designs that decorated the walls of El Navajo, the Harvey Company hotel in Gallup, New Mexico, and he participated in the house blessing ceremony which was part of the hotel's opening activities in 1923. In 1924 Miguelito was in Albuquerque to work on a special commission for J. F. Huckel. Under the direction of Herman Schweizer, Miguelito drew several sandpaintings and recounted the stories to accompany each one. The story of Miguelito's life, his sandpaintings, and their stories were published in Gladys Reichard's *Navajo Medicine Man*. Miguelito's story as told by Reichard is still in print today, retitled *Navajo Medicine Man Sandpaintings* and reprinted by Dover Press in 1993. The original forty-four sandpaintings Miguelito created for J. F. Huckel are in the collections of the Colorado Springs Fine Arts Museum.

LA POSADA: WINSLOW, ARIZONA

La Posada (The Resting Place) opened its doors in Winslow, Arizona in 1930. The 68,000-square-foot hotel was built as a replica of an old Spanish rancho:

> *The floors are of oak, pegged and grooved, and laid in random widths. . . . Each of the eighty guest chambers, including five suites differs from the others; the draperies are designed in colors to match the painted desert, and the floors are covered with Indian rugs, old designs. . . . In the lobby, corridors and stair landings are numerous pieces of ancient workmanship, an old Mexican implement box, several monk chairs and chests and benches. The grounds embrace eight acres in which eight car-loads of shrubbery have been planted thus providing a spacious garden with flowers, shrubbery, vines and inviting seats. . . . This provides only a fleeting glimpse of the new jewel in the Harvey System's chain of fine hostelries. . . .*
> —ROGER WILLIAMS BIRDSEYE, The Santa Fe Magazine, 1930

H.4224 LA POSADA, FRED HARVEY HOTEL, WINSLOW, ARIZONA

Postcard of La Posada

Said to be Harvey Company architect Mary Jane Colter's favorite hotel, La Posada was a Harveycar base. From the hotel, travelers could take special motor cruises to the Grand Canyon, Flagstaff, Prescott, or Phoenix, White Mountain Apache country, Hopi Villages, Rainbow Bridge, Canyon de Chelly, and other interesting locations.

Many Harvey Company hotels, including The Alvarado Hotel in Albuquerque, have been razed. Edifices with lovely sounding names such as El Ortiz in Lamy, New Mexico, the Escalante in Seligman, Arizona, and El Navajo in Gallup, New Mexico, remain only in memories and on colorful postcards and brochures published by the Harvey Company.

EL NAVAJO: GALLUP, NEW MEXICO

In 1922, when plans were being made for a new Fred Harvey Hotel in Gallup, New Mexico, Mary Jane Colter, by then well known for her architectural designs, suggested Navajo sandpainting designs for the hotel lobby. A search began for authentic copies of Navajo sandpaintings, leading the company to buy a collection of designs on paper from Sam Day, Jr., of St. Michaels, Arizona. Fred Harvey artist Fred Geary, aided by Navajo medicine man Miguelito, reproduced some sandpaintings from the Day collection on the walls of El Navajo. On the day of its opening, Miguelito and twenty-nine other Navajo medicine men blessed the hotel.

Miguelito had spent almost two years in 1915 working for the Fred Harvey Company in its Painted Desert and Grand Canyon exhibits. He shared much of his knowledge with Gladys Reichard, an anthropologist from Barnard College of Columbia University. Reichard spent several summers researching Navajo culture, living with Miguelito's family during part of the research period.

When J. F. Huckel died in 1936, his widow, Minnie, thought it would be a fitting tribute to her deceased husband to publish his collection of Navajo sandpaintings. She retained Reichard to write *Navajo Medicine Man*, which was published by J. J. Augustin Company in 1939.

El Navajo Hotel was constructed in 1922 in Gallup, New Mexico

Santa Fe de-Luxe

The only extra-fare train via any line Chicago and California

CHAPTER 7

PROMOTING *the* SOUTHWEST *in* PICTURES *and* PRINT

1903 Postcard of Isleta Pueblo woman

OPPOSITE
Santa Fe Railway advertisement from
McClure's, February 1912

Art prints will be published and thousands made for sale along the Santa Fe . . . "Picture Rooms" are now to be established along the line with a view to offering the travelling public photographs and paintings of typical southwestern objects.
—ALBUQUERQUE JOURNAL-DEMOCRAT, *April 2, 1903*

Publications played a critical role in the Santa Fe Railway and Harvey Company's jointly developed and executed, very successful strategy to promote tourism in the Southwest. Between 1892, when the Santa Fe Railroad published the first booklet on the Grand Canyon, and November 1930, when the last Harveycar Indian Detours booklet appeared, both companies generated a flood of enduring and ephemeral pieces promoting the region's wonders: more than 110 books, booklets, and brochures. Publications were promotional in nature, and many contain information written by scholars such as John Wesley Powell, George Dorsey, and others who had studied and worked in the Southwest. In September 1926 when he extolled the Santa Fe/Harvey Company campaign to advertise the new Indian Detours, its publicist Roger Williams Birdseye claimed that "Some two million pieces of Santa Fe printed matter are absorbed annually by the general public."

OPPOSITE

The Fred Harvey Company and the
Santa Fe Railway collaborated to produce
a number of books in the early 1900s.

In 1892 the Santa Fe Railroad began publicity for southern California and the Grand Canyon as part of preparations for the Chicago World's Columbian Exposition and the inauguration of its first luxury passenger train, the California Limited. Assistant passenger agent Charles A. Higgins was active in these early promotions. W. F. White was traffic manager of the railroad before it was reorganized as the Atchison, Topeka & Santa Fe Railway, and in 1896 he was encouraged by the new president Edward P. Ripley to develop more innovative advertising campaigns. After Higgins' death in 1900, Ripley appointed William H. Simpson, a former newspaperman who was a clerk in the General Passenger Department, to become the Santa Fe's general advertising agent, a post he held until his death in 1933. Unlike Huckel, Herman Schweizer had no publishing experience but was considered to have a keen eye for attractive publications as well as an understanding of what the traveling public would buy.

With the Santa Fe's Simpson, Huckel and Schweizer launched a multifaceted publishing venture that lasted some forty years. Santa Fe and Fred Harvey publications, sometimes jointly issued, range from a lengthy anthropological work like George M. Dorsey's 223-page *Indians of the Southwest* (1903) to short, informative brochures and pamphlets and virtually text-free souvenir volumes of photographs. Published by the Santa Fe Railway, the overt purpose of Dorsey's book was to encourage travel to the Southwest by describing the lives, artwork, and ceremonies of its Native peoples while the covert purpose was to promote sales of Native American material in the Harvey Company facilities. Through his own field experiences and those of his colleagues, it was possible for Dorsey to develop this extensive softcover book which sold for fifty cents.

Diverging from the title of his book, Dorsey chose to introduce the Southwest via the southern Plains. The sections pertaining to the Plains contained extensive written material about the Osage and the Arapaho, two groups of people well known to Dorsey because of his field work among them. Not only did writing about the Plains allow Dorsey to draw upon familiar material, it also enabled him to feature two cultural groups whose objects had been collected by the Indian Department and were available for sale.

FIRST FAMILIES OF THE SOUTHWEST

AMERICAN INDIANS

FIRST FAMILIES OF
THE SOUTHWEST

AMERICAN
INDIANS
FIRST FAMILIES OF
THE SOUTHWEST

THE GREAT SOUTHWEST

Santa Fe
Harveycars

Indian-detours
—Most distinctive Motor Cruise
service in the world

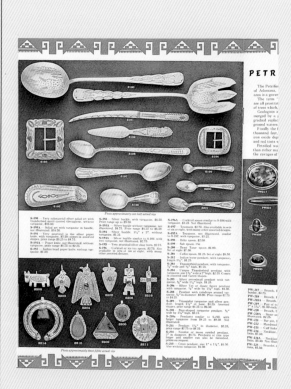

This 1938 mail-order catalog was
the only one the Harvey Company produced.

Similarly, Dorsey devoted a large section of the book to a description of California peoples, another area in which the Indian Department maintained collections for sale. Dorsey had access to information about California through Dr. John Hudson's research and incorporated Hudson's written material in the book.

The southwestern section of *Indians of the Southwest* relied heavily on material about the Hopi people, a subject H. R. Voth had researched and wrote about extensively. The *Albuquerque Journal-Democrat* favorably reviewed the book on September 17, 1903:

> The book is valuable and should be placed in more substantial form than the paper cover with which the Santa Fe has supplied it.

The Harvey Company employed the services of others in addition to Dorsey and Voth to write ethnological books, brochures, and articles. Antonio Apache was one individual hired by the Harvey Company who provided such a service; he served in some capacity as directed by Dorsey at the 1893 Field Columbian Exposition. It is likely that Dorsey introduced Antonio Apache to the members of the Harvey Company Indian Department at The Alvarado Hotel. While there in 1903, he wrote an article that appeared in a Chicago newspaper:

> The Sunday Chicago Record Herald of May 3rd published a most interesting and instructive article on "Indian Artists of the Great Southwest and Their Work," written by Antonio Apache, an ethnologist of wide-spread fame, who is now a guest of the Harvey Curio here, for the purpose of carrying on his studies. (May 8)

In 1919 Schweizer was actively interested in "something to take the place of *Indians of the Southwest*" and outlined what such a book should include. However, except for Huckel's editions of *American Indians: First Families of the Southwest* and the Indian Detours materials, it is usually impossible to trace Simpson's, Huckel's or Schweizer's involvement with a particular publication.

To further develop credible written publicity, the Fred Harvey Company and the Santa Fe Railway sought relations with the colony of writers in Santa Fe and Taos, New Mexico. After 1915, northern New Mexico enjoyed an influx of writers who moved

Postcard of Isleta girls selling miniaturized pottery, early 1900s

into the area, and they began to chronicle life in that part of the world. Taos and Santa Fe had already welcomed artists; writers were now drawn to the area and soon a literary community was formed. Extended visits to the area were paid by D. H. Lawrence, Willa Cather, Robert Frost, Thornton Wilder, Carl Sandburg, John Galsworthy, Sinclair Lewis, and Edna St. Vincent Millay. Writers residing in the community included Mabel Dodge Luhan, Alice Corbin Henderson, Witter Bynner, Mary Austin, Haniel Long, and Oliver LaFarge. In 1928, the Santa Fe Railway published a booklet entitled *They Know New Mexico: Intimate Sketches by Western Writers.* Contributors included Charles Lummis, Alice Corbin Henderson, Mary Austin, Witter Bynner, Elizabeth Willis DeHuff, and others.

Herman Schweizer and Mary Austin became friends, exchanging letters in 1930. Schweizer wrote to Austin on April 8 of that year:

> *Since the meeting in Santa Fe I presume I may call you friend.*
> *I appreciate very much your kindness in sending me the book, and I would like to know whether or not we are selling these at our news stands, and if not, I will look into it and see that some of them are placed on sale.*

Austin responded on November 18:

> *I was just on the point of writing you to thank you for the help you so kindly, and so delightfully, afforded me for my next novel. It is difficult for me some-times to make my male characters come alive and appear in the round. I do not promise you that you will recognize my hero in print. . . . . . At the same time, do not be surprised at strange, secret resemblances that were never communicated to me in words. Genius has its own way of getting at the truth.*

As Schweizer mentioned in his letter to Austin, the Harvey Company and the Santa Fe Railway stocked a large collection of regional books in their newsstands, another means of promoting travel to the Southwest. A small book catalogue from 1940 shows the large and eclectic selection of books available for sale.

As well as making publications available to the traveling public through their news-stands, the Harvey Company kept three reference libraries stocked with regional and related material. A catalogue of holdings—a thirty-page list compiled in 1927—indicates that reference libraries were kept at three locations: the Albuquerque Indian Storeroom Library, the Hopi House Library and the Bright Angel Bookcase Library at the Grand Canyon. The listing reflects the scholarly, ethnographic, and popular nature of the collection.

Paintings were another opportunity to bring the public's attention to railroad travel to the Southwest. To encourage travelers to select its route over those of the Union Pacific, the Northern Pacific, and other competitors, the Santa Fe began to commission paintings depicting the Southwest's spectacular landscapes. Capitalizing on the American artists who were fleeing the confusion of city life in the late 1800s and forming artist colonies in the suburbs of eastern cities and in the American Southwest, the Santa Fe Railway hired them to depict the natural wonders of the West, such as the Grand Canyon, as well as the exotic image of the West via its native inhabitants. Artistic renderings were used in numerous promotional forms including annual calendars and railroad advertisements. The Fred Harvey Company also used the artists' paintings on menu covers, postcards, and small books about Native Americans. Thomas Moran, Louis Akin, and E. Irving Couse were among many noted artists whose canvases captured the Southwest for the Santa Fe.

Postcard of Louis Akin's painting of El Tovar

The Santa Fe Railway's interest in paintings began in 1896, when Edward P. Ripley became president of the company. Ripley encouraged W. F. White, traffic manager, to study the possibilities of advertising for the Santa Fe Railway, which had just escaped bankruptcy following the depression of 1893. White developed a successful advertising campaign. His first success was to purchase all rights to a painting, *Grand Canyon*, just completed by Western artist Thomas Moran and to have chromolithographs, or color prints, made. These images were placed in golden frames. A gilt plaque rested at the bottom of each frame identifying the scene, the artist, and the Santa Fe Railway. Thousands of the chromolithographs were

6848. PUEBLO INDIANS SELLING POTTERY.
COPYRIGHT, 1902, BY DETROIT PHOTOGRAPHIC CO.

Images were manipulated by the Harvey Company and Santa Fe Railway to satisfy tourists' expectations. The conductors in the postcard, top, were painted to look like Pueblo women.

made and distributed across the land. Many were displayed in Santa Fe Railway depots. Moran was provided a round-trip ticket to the Southwest along with food and lodging for a period of time, for which he provided the Santa Fe Railway with paintings that could be used to advertise the Southwest.

Other well-known artists willing to capture Southwestern scenes on canvas were employed by the Fred Harvey Company and the Santa Fe Railway. In 1906 Louis Akin painted *El Tovar Hotel, Grand Canyon* for the Santa Fe. Like other artists, Akin had first come west on an offer from Simpson to paint Southwestern landscapes and Native people.

From its early beginnings with paintings by artists such as Moran and Akin, the Santa Fe Railway collection of fine art blossomed. Throughout the years works of other prominent artists became part of the Santa Fe Railway's corporate art collection. By 1907, advertising agent William H. Simpson had acquired 108 paintings for the Santa Fe Railway. Works by Frank Paul Sauerwein, E. A. Burbank, E. Irving Couse, Ernest L. Blumenschein, William R. Leigh, Bert Geer Phillips, E. Martin Hennings, and other talented artists hold a place in the Santa Fe Railway's corporate collection in Schaumburg, Illinois, today.

Seemingly endless advertisements—small, colorful brochures, albums, postcards, matchbook covers, menus, and posters—were also produced by the Santa Fe Railway and the Fred Harvey Company. All beautifully executed, each one advertised visions and views to be enjoyed during the train trip west.

Picture postcards became immensely popular by the early 1900s. While giving friends and family at home a vision of what had been seen and experienced, a tourist could jot down a colorful message sharing the Western experience, as in a postcard written in 1907.

"Just a line from the most wonderful place in the world"

October 8, 1907. This is the hotel and Indian Bldg and station all put up by the Santa Fe Ry. The rest of the architecture of the town is scarcely of this elaborate order. We arrived

on a carnival day; saw the governor and a U.S. General and a troop of cavalry.
Also plenty of natives and Indians. I am standing the journey very well G.B.L.

The Harvey Company produced numerous postcards promoting the Southwest, many of them containing photographs or sketches of the Harvey Company hotels that emphasized the grandeur of the buildings. In some of the sketches, like one of The Alvarado Hotel, the actual length of the building complex was exaggerated to provide an illusion of expansion.

The postcards were first printed by the Detroit Publishing Company. Later, the Fred Harvey "Photostint" emblem was trademarked and displayed on the back of the card.

Many postcards and books featured images of Native peoples as anonymous representatives of the Southwest, but even during the early years, the Hopi-Tewa potter Nampeyo and Navajo weaver Elle of Ganado were featured by name.

In addition to developing marketing concepts for the Harvey Company, Huckel and Schweizer also researched and created some of the products. In 1908, Schweizer visited the Abo Cliffs site, near Mountainair, New Mexico.

Just north of the tracks near Mountainair, Schweizer left the train and hiked up to a south-facing overhang. He noticed pictographs on the roof of an alcove noted earlier by archaeologists Adolph Bandelier and Jesse Walter Fewkes. Schweizer sketched several of the designs he saw on the rock walls. Two of them particularly impressed him: the thunderbird and the star frog. He returned with his drawings to Albuquerque and wrote of them to Huckel in Kansas City. After receiving Huckel's approval, the Abo thunderbird and the star frog were used on the Indian Department stationery beginning in 1908 and was copyrighted in 1909. The star frog image appeared for a short time on the letterhead. However, the thunderbird became the company's logo and was widely used in publications and on silver jewelry. Using Schweizer's sketches, Harvey artist Fred Geary painted the thunderbird on the ceiling of The Watchtower at the Grand Canyon in 1933.

Schweizer and Huckel elicited the expertise of museum professionals to produce a handout for tourists describing the origin of the thunderbird with the logo pictured.

The thunderbird image was used extensively by the Fred Harvey Company and was copyrighted by them in 1909.

RIGHT
Silver jewelry sold to tourists by the
Fred Harvey Company was lightweight and
often contained images of arrows and
the thunderbird.

OPPOSITE
Playing cards produced by the Fred Harvey
Company in 1911. Only the Navajo weaver
Elle of Ganado and Hopi-Tewa potter
Nampeyo were mentioned by name.

Huckel wrote to Dr. George Pepper, curator at the American Museum of Natural History in New York, and Charles Owen, curator at the Field Columbian Museum in Chicago, for information about the thunderbird. When the information was received, Huckel produced a several-page story about the thunderbird, reflecting word-for-word information provided by Pepper and Owens. Schweizer revised the information, producing a short consolidated story of the thunderbird, which was used on the handout.

In 1911 the Harvey Company produced another marketing item: decks of playing cards that were distributed by the Santa Fe Railway. At least two different decks of playing cards were printed and the backs of each were different. One set showed the Zuni knife-wing bird and the other, a reproduction of a painting by Frank Paul Sauerwein, which appeared on the cover of the book *The Great Southwest*. The face of each deck was also different. The knife-wing bird deck predominantly included images of Native peoples while the other deck included hotels and landscapes as well as Native peoples. Nampeyo and Elle of Ganado are the only two artists represented whose names are printed on the playing cards. All others are anonymous.

Sales to tourists also fell as the Great Depression took its toll on discretionary income. In 1938 the Indian Department resorted to a widely distributed mail-order catalogue to revive sales. This was the first and only direct sales venture in the history of the company. The catalogue featured inexpensive jewelry, spoons, knives, and other reasonably priced items. A few of the older, rare objects were also shown.

CHAPTER 8

THE GRAND CANYON

*This is getting farther yet from the Desert—but it too has its charms.
. . . It's full of beauty in many ways—but I can't believe the most inspir-
ing of it can bring to one anything like the awe that the Canyon
inspires—it can't hold me indefinitely as the Canyon can.*
—ARTIST LOUIS AKIN TO WILLIAM H. SIMPSON,
October 14, 1909, writing from British Columbia

In 1901, The Santa Fe Railway rebuilt the sixty-five miles of track
from Williams, Arizona, to the Grand Canyon. The original line
to the Grand Canyon had been plagued with a soft roadbed. The
Santa Fe, undeterred by small obstacles such as this, had "located a mountain,
which is almost a solid heap of volcanic rock. This rock will be used as a foundation for
the track all the way and will make the best roadbed possible" (*The Williams News*, March
25, 1905).

   El Tovar, the Santa Fe's luxury hotel designed by Charles Whittlesey, opened on
November 1, 1904, and Hopi House opened January 5, 1905. Many Americans of the
early 1900s had become disenchanted with the mechanized look of goods produced by

*Harvey Company menu with the Grand
Canyon on the cover, c. 1940*

OPPOSITE
Harveycars at the Grand Canyon, early 1900s

June 1909 advertisement in McClure's
for the Grand Canyon

the industrial revolution and sought handcrafted items. The arts and crafts movement introduced a style of architecture and decor—a look of dark, handmade natural woods and homey handcrafted Victorian clutter. The Harvey Company, and its architect and decorator, Mary Jane Colter, used this style for the interiors of the Alvarado and El Tovar hotels, Hopi House, and other Harvey Company properties.

While J. F. Huckel remained in Albuquerque to oversee Indian Department activities, Herman Schweizer went to other Harvey Company locations to establish new Indian Department branches. By 1905, Schweizer was managing new operations at Williams, Arizona, and at Hopi House at the South Rim of the Grand Canyon. The front page of *The Williams News*, for Saturday, March 25, 1905 reported:

Manager Herman Switzer, of the Fred Harvey curio Department in this city returned from a stay of ten days or so at the Hotel El Tovar, at The Grand Canyon.

Colter based the design for Hopi House on a building from the village of Oraibi. Through Hopi House, Colter attempted to replicate a pueblo-style dwelling and the Harvey Company developed another primary enterprise that elaborated the worlds' fair plan. Here, the Harvey Company provided accommodations at the site of a natural wonder of the Southwest, the Grand Canyon, while simultaneously offering tourists an opportunity to view people of another culture either creating craft arts or performing dances. Introduced as an educational and entertaining experience, *El Tovar, Grand Canyon of Arizona* describes Hopi House:

Several rooms in the Hopi House are devoted to an exhibit of rare and costly specimens of Indian and Mexican handiwork. Here is displayed the priceless Harvey collection of old Navajo blankets, winner of a grand prize at the Louisiana Purchase Exposition; and finally, a salesroom containing the most interesting display of genuine Indian and Mexican handiwork in this country, gathered from all sections of the Southwest and Northwest.

MARY JANE COLTER

TOURISTS VISITING THE GRAND CANYON today find they are surrounded by evidence of Mary Jane Colter's (1869–1958) architectural work. Hopi House, the Lookout, Hermit's Rest, The Watchtower and Phantom Ranch all bear testament to this remarkable woman. Talented, hard-working and strong willed, Mary Jane Colter accepted a contract assignment with the Fred Harvey Company in 1902. Her task was to decorate the newly built Alvarado Hotel and its adjacent Indian Museum, artist demonstration room, and sales room.

Colter's next assignment with the Harvey Company was to design Hopi House. Her design was based on a building she had visited at Oraibi. She supervised the building of the pueblo structure, which was constructed by Hopi workmen.  Mennonite missionary and Hopi ethnographer Henry R. Voth assisted Colter by providing cultural information for the project.

In 1910, at the age of forty, Mary Jane Colter was again called into service by the Harvey Company, this time as a full-time employee. Her assignment was to design and decorate Fred Harvey hotels and restaurants. Her supervisor was J. F. Huckel, though unpublished Harvey family records indicate that it was Minnie Harvey Huckel who was Colter's mentor. Architectural design and decoration was an unusual occupation for a Victorian lady of Colter's day, and the support of an influential Harvey member was a definite asset.

In 1910, Colter decorated El Ortiz Hotel in Lamy, New Mexico, then continued on to the Grand Canyon where the largest existing examples of her work can still be seen. In 1925, she decorated the Fred Harvey shops in Union Station in Chicago, then went to Santa Fe to refurbish the newly acquired La Fonda Hotel. Colter designed and decorated La Posada hotel in Winslow, Arizona. La Posada opened in 1930 and is said to have been Colter's favorite project. Like many of the railroad hotels, La Posada stretches along the railroad tracks displaying welcoming arches, buff-colored stucco and tiled roof.

Months of research were undertaken, some of it with Herman Schweizer, before Colter completed the design for the Watchtower at the Grand Canyon. Built in 1933, it reflected the Anasazi towers of the Four Corners area of Arizona, New Mexico, Colorado, and Utah. She continued her work at the Canyon in 1935 when she designed and decorated Bright Angel Lodge and shortly thereafter the men's and women's dormitories. In 1947 she decorated the Painted Desert Inn surrounded by the Petrified Forest. The murals she commissioned Fred Kabotie to paint on the walls are still visible today. Other assignments include Colter's work at Union Stations in Kansas City, St. Louis, and Los Angeles.

In later years Colter continued to work and stayed in close contact with Harvey family members. She retired to Santa Fe and built a small house for herself not far from the Plaza. Mary Jane Colter passed away in Santa Fe in 1958.

Schweizer's responsibilities as manager of the Indian Department facilities away from Albuquerque headquarters included day-to-day business matters, building maintenance problems, and human relations challenges. Schweizer found himself handling a multitude of problems such as, on February 14, 1905, fixing a leaky Hopi House roof. Keeping a full complement of Native American artisans at work in Albuquerque and at Hopi House was by itself a full-time job. Most Native Americans had ceremonial and family responsibilities at home that conflicted with Harvey Company interests in full-time employees. Huckel and Schweizer again depended upon J. L. Hubbell of Ganado to make arrangements for Hopi and Navajo people to work. Several letters reflect the intensity of the Harvey Company in securing artist-demonstrators:

> *A silversmith is quite an attraction, and, as I wrote to you, I would like to have one.* (HUCKEL TO J. L. HUBBELL, April 26, 1905)

> *We find that our sale of silver falls off when there is no silversmith.* (HUCKEL TO HUBBELL, June 26, 1905)

> *Get some Indians to the Canyon at once.* (SCHWEIZER TO HUBBELL, September 13, 1905)

The Hopi-Tewa potter Nampeyo was the star attraction at Hopi House at the Grand Canyon when it opened. Present at Hopi House five days after the opening, Nampeyo began demonstrating potterymaking on January 10, 1905, and continued her work through April 1905. Nampeyo and her daughter Annie demonstrated potterymaking while Nampeyo's sons and

PAUL SAUFKIE

PAUL SAUFKIE WAS BORN in the Hopi village of Shungopovi on August 20, 1898. Around 1935 he moved to the Grand Canyon to work for the Fred Harvey Company where he demonstrated silver making techniques. The Harvey Company was anxious to have a silversmith employed because it significantly increased jewelry sales. It was during his brief employment that Saufkie agreed to be the subject of a series of photographs for the production of a Harvey Company postcard.

Saufkie worked for the Harvey Company only for one or two years. He left the Canyon to work for Reece Vaughn at Vaughn's Indian Store in Phoenix. In the 1940s, Saufkie had returned to Shungopovi, where he developed the silver overlay technique typical of Hopi jewelry today.

This silver and turquoise pendant, 2" diameter, made by Paul Saufkie, was collected by Mary Jane Colter.

OPPOSITE
Hopi employee Paul Saufkie was asked to pose as a Navajo silversmith by the Harvey Company for postcards. This image was hand tinted by another Hopi employee, Porter Timeche.

Hopi House in 1950.
American Indian Art Magazine

husband performed dances for the visiting tourists. By employing Nampeyo's family, the Harvey Company obtained a dual attraction.

In letters written by J. F. Huckel on March 23 and March 26, 1905, to Ganado Indian trader J. L. Hubbell, Huckel writes: "Will you please write Mr. Schweizer at the Grand Canyon where he is manager for present," and "Mr. Schweizer is manager of Hopi House and I have given him transportation for Nampeyo's party." Within a week of the Hopi House opening, Schweizer wrote to J. L. Hubbell: "I find that the Indians brought only two small boxes of clay for Nampeyo to make pottery. This clay will only last her a very short time, and she is anxious to have the same clay she has been accustomed to, and I think she is right, otherwise she will not be able to turn out as good pottery" (January 10, 1905). Schweizer, through Hubbell, arranged for clay to be collected and shipped to the Canyon.

By the time of Harvey Company employment, Nampeyo was already well known to anthropologists and photographers of the Southwest and had become firmly established as a significant pueblo potter. Unlike Elle of Ganado, whose star status was developed by the Harvey Company, Nampeyo achieved this status on her own and was promoted by the Harvey Company because of the attention she had already acquired.

Known for the low-shouldered jars and intricate designs derived from prehistoric Sikyatki polychromes, Nampeyo's work was distinctive from that of other potters at the turn of the century.

Many anthropologists debate the origin of the Sikyatki revival begun by Nampeyo. Some contend that she copied designs from pottery sherds at the excavation site of Sikyatki in 1895 and 1896 at Fewkes' suggestion. Others believe that Nampeyo had an interest in the ancient pottery sherds before the excavations and that she collected the sherds before Fewkes' arrival.

Fewkes was not alone in his recognition of Nampeyo and the pottery she created. As

NAMPEYO

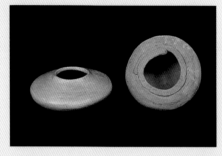

"discs" by Harvey Company head J. F. Huckel because of their dramatic shapes. Her pottery came to the attention of many anthropologists and she was widely photographed with the extraordinary jars and bowls she created. As early as 1903 Nampeyo was providing information about potterymaking to anthropologist George H. Pepper and in the 1920s to Ruth Bunzel for her book *The Pueblo Potter*.

The Harvey Company employed Nampeyo on two occasions at Hopi House at the Grand Canyon and sent her to Chicago on behalf of the company. Special tags were made for her pottery. She and her work were pictured in many Harvey Company publications and her picture was circulated widely on postcards and playing cards.

BORN AROUND 1862 in the Hopi village of Hano, the Tewa potter Nampeyo received much acclaim in her lifetime. So adept was Nampeyo at her art at a time when pottery production had declined, that archaeologist J. W. Fewkes feared her pottery would be mistaken for the Sikyatki wares removed from the prehistoric site.

Nampeyo revived the style of the low-shouldered jars of the Sikyatki period. Her pottery jars were called

Top: Nampeyo demonstrated potterymaking at the Grand Canyon in 1905 and 1907. This unfired series, 5", may have been made at that time.
Bottom: jar by Nampeyo, 2 1/2", early 1900s

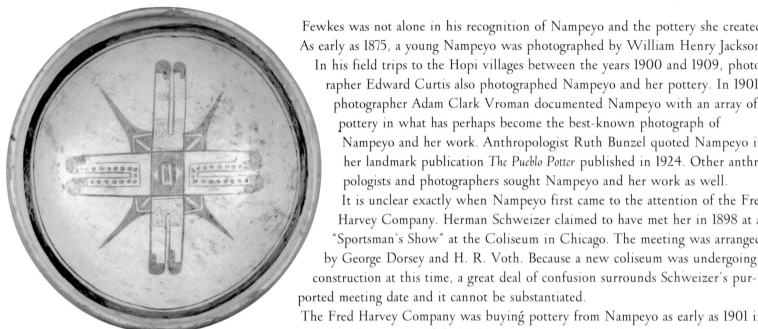

Bowl by Nampeyo, 10" diameter, early 1900s

Fewkes was not alone in his recognition of Nampeyo and the pottery she created. As early as 1875, a young Nampeyo was photographed by William Henry Jackson. In his field trips to the Hopi villages between the years 1900 and 1909, photographer Edward Curtis also photographed Nampeyo and her pottery. In 1901, photographer Adam Clark Vroman documented Nampeyo with an array of pottery in what has perhaps become the best-known photograph of Nampeyo and her work. Anthropologist Ruth Bunzel quoted Nampeyo in her landmark publication *The Pueblo Potter* published in 1924. Other anthropologists and photographers sought Nampeyo and her work as well.

It is unclear exactly when Nampeyo first came to the attention of the Fred Harvey Company. Herman Schweizer claimed to have met her in 1898 at a "Sportsman's Show" at the Coliseum in Chicago. The meeting was arranged by George Dorsey and H. R. Voth. Because a new coliseum was undergoing construction at this time, a great deal of confusion surrounds Schweizer's purported meeting date and it cannot be substantiated.

The Fred Harvey Company was buying pottery from Nampeyo as early as 1901 in preparation for the opening of the Indian Department at the Alvarado in 1902. Fewkes noted the sales dimension of Nampeyo's pottery in stating: "The extent of her work, for which there was a large demand, may be judged by the great numbers of Hopi bowls displayed in every Harvey store from New Mexico to California." (Fewkes' 1911–1912 33rd *Annual Report of the Bureau of American Ethnology*) Nampeyo's pottery was sought and collected by Harvey Company employees as well, including Mary Jane Colter in 1904 and 1905.

Nampeyo's pottery designs were so appealing that they were used in Fred Harvey Company published brochures. One bowl made by Nampeyo and collected by Colter while she was employed by the Harvey Company in 1904 was later used as the cover of four Harvey Company brochures. One of these, titled *Christmas Gifts*, was produced to advertise Native arts and crafts sold by the Fred Harvey Company at 225 Michigan Avenue in Chicago. The bowl also appeared on the cover of an untitled promotional mailing for Hopi House. The design was not credited to Nampeyo and the bowl remained in Colter's collection until the collection was bequeathed to Mesa Verde National Park.

Mary Jane Colter's collection information for the bowl indicates that she acquired it in 1904. If Colter's collection data is accurate, she was purchasing pottery directly from Nampeyo before Nampeyo began her work as an artist-demonstrator at Hopi House. It is possible that Colter purchased pottery from Nampeyo while researching and planning the design of Hopi House.

The image of the bowl was used on two other small brochures. One contained twenty pages of photographs and text about Harvey Company facilities at Albuquerque and the Grand Canyon. The bowl image appears on the back cover while an image of the thunderbird appears on the last interior page and the Zuni knife-wing bird on the first interior page. Although not dated, the brochure was probably produced after 1909, the year the Harvey Company acquired copyright for the thunderbird. The fourth brochure was titled *The Indian and Mexican Building* and was produced for the California Limited Westbound. In a manner similar to other brochures, Nampeyo's bowl was on the front cover and the Zuni knife-wing bird was on the back cover. Like the thunderbird, which was used on Harvey Company stationery and in jewelry, and the knife wing bird, which was used on stationery and appeared in a sign above the Indian Department Building in Albuquerque, Nampeyo's bowl became a logo for the Harvey Company.

During the same year that Nampeyo was demonstrating potterymaking at the Grand Canyon, trader J. L. Hubbell was marketing Nampeyo's pottery in his sales catalogue. The 1905 catalogue shows a front and side view of her pottery and reads: "Nampea pottery; the only pottery that compares with the old in color, finish and design." As with the Harvey publications, no other potters are mentioned by name in Hubbell's sales catalogue. Although the catalogue included pottery, textiles, baskets, and kachina dolls made by Hopi people; textiles, jewelry, and baskets made by Navajo people; baskets made by Pima people; and an array of miscellaneous objects including bows and arrows, no artists other than Nampeyo are mentioned by name.

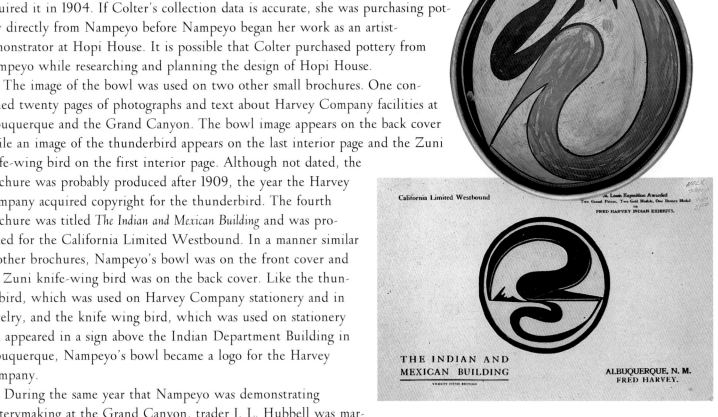

This bowl, 9" diameter, was purchased from Nampeyo in 1904 by Mary Jane Colter and used on the cover of four brochures produced by the Fred Harvey Company.

Nampeyo and family members at
Hopi House, 1905

In 1907, Nampeyo demonstrated potterymaking again at the Grand Canyon. The Harvey Company was interested not only in having Nampeyo and her family return to the Canyon but also in having children accompany her. Huckel wrote to Hubbell on October 24, 1905, that children were an attraction for the tourists: "Of course, the children are one of the chief attractions to the traveling public."
During the time that Nampeyo worked for the Harvey Company, special black, gold, and white stickers were produced that read "Made by Nampeyo, Hopi" and placed on her pottery. Such a sticker remains on one of the bowls purchased from Nampeyo by Mary Jane Colter at the Grand Canyon in 1905. The bowl is in the collection of Mesa Verde National Park.

The Harvey Company also bought Nampeyo's pottery through J. L. Hubbell requesting specifically either bowls or the low-shoulder jars which J. F. Huckel referred to as "discs." Although the company retained few examples of Nampeyo's work, Huckel acquired a jar around 1905 to 1910 for his personal collection, which he later considered giving to the Harvey Company Museum. The jar remained in his collection until his death, was given to Katherine Harvey by Minnie Harvey Huckel, and given by Katherine Harvey to the Nelson-Atkins Museum of Art.

Nampeyo was not the only attraction at Hopi House: Its architectural charms beckoned visitors to a showroom and a sales room similar to those at The Alvarado Hotel Indian Building. The collections H. R. Voth amassed, including those that had been displayed at the Louisiana Purchase Exposition in 1904 in St. Louis, were key to the display at Hopi House. More than 400 objects exhibited in St. Louis were moved to Hopi House where they remained until sold to Clark Wissler of the American Museum of Natural History by D. F. Smith, manager of the sales shop at Hopi House on May 20, 1910. Notes with the acquisition read:

> *From private information it seems that Mr. Voth gradually accumulated this lot during his ten years' residence among the Hopi and while he labored partly in the interest of the*

Field Museum. *When he left the Hopi country he found it a burden on his hands and sold it to "Fred Harvey" with the understanding that it should never be broken or used for anything but museum purposes. . . . The purchase of the collection by the American Museum was possibly chiefly because of the conviction of Mr. D. E. Smith, Manager of Hopi House, that such things should be in a large public museum and not in private or commercial hands.*

Although Smith may have felt strongly that Voth's collection of Hopi material should be in the possession of a museum rather than a commercial business such as Hopi House, Huckel was disappointed at the loss of the material and in 1910 hired Voth to build another collection. The collection was completed in 1912 and accompanied by a small catalogue written by Voth and titled *The Henry R. Voth Hopi Indian Collection at Grand Canyon, Arizona.*

Hopi canteens, 7"–9" diameter, late 1800s, sold by the Fred Harvey Company to the Nelson-Atkins Museum in 1933

At the Grand Canyon, we lived there for 27 years. Fred Harvey ran the Alvarado Hotel, the Bright Angel, the Hopi House, and, of course, the cafeterias. . . . I worked there for awhile [as a Harvey girl].

Oh, there was a bunch of us Indian girls that worked there [the Grand Canyon] at the hotel, in the rooms—cleaning, and of course, a lot of them worked in the dining room as waitresses. . . . I know two of my sisters were going to college and they used to go down just to make a little money and in the fall they'd come back to go to school.

It was sort of fun, you know. There was always Indian dances performed at the Hopi House, men with bonnets on. Oh, there was just too many tourists around there.

—ELIZABETH ARKIE, *Laguna Pueblo,*
  Age 72, 1995

In front of the west wall of Hopi House stand (from left) Santa Fe Railway passenger agent E. B. Duffy, Herman Schweizer, Leo Humequaftewa, Professor Einstein, Mrs. Einstein, Lucy Timeche, an unidentified Navajo child, Chester Dennis, and Porter Timeche (with drum).

El Tovar and Hopi House continued to be strong drawing points for tourists while the Canyon itself offered an enchanting vista. Several well-known Americans visited the Canyon, including scientist Albert Einstein, President Theodore Roosevelt, and President William Howard Taft. The Canyon was a primary area for Harvey Company development as evidenced by the Watchtower, designed by Mary Jane Colter and built in 1933. Many Native Americans, particularly Hopi people from the village of Shungopovi, worked at the Canyon in varying capacities.

The Grand Canyon became a National Park in 1919. However, the dedication did not take place until April 30, 1920. El Tovar and Hopi House and the outdoor space between them were the stage and the Canyon was the backdrop for the play that took place the day of the dedication and on many other less auspicious occasions. Events took place both inside El Tovar and in front of Hopi House. In an April 24, 1920 letter to J. F. Huckel, Herman Schweizer wrote of the script that had been prepared for the Harvey Indian participants in the Grand Canyon National Park dedication program to be held at El Tovar:

> *The speakers are to address the audience from the balcony where the large Moose head is located. While the main lobby facing the speaker will probably not hold more than about four hundred, the entire lobby floor, including the mezzanine, should comfortably hold in the neighborhood of one thousand persons within easy reach of the speaker's voice. When we discussed this matter at Kansas City I think we were agreed that it seemed necessary to find some more serious side of the Indian entertainment so it would properly fit in with this dedication ceremony. After talking with the Indians, I think I have found the missing link.*

SAM PEMAUHYE

KNOWN TO MANY VISITORS to the Grand Canyon as Hopi Sam, Sam Pemauhye had a long career with the Fred Harvey Company. Before he began his employment at the Canyon, Pemauhye worked for about ten years for the Santa Fe Railway in the Santa Fe area.

During part of his employment, Pemauhye worked as a porter and shined shoes at the Bright Angel Lodge. He also entertained visitors to Lookout Studio on the South Rim by telling stories. He was present for the Watchtower dedication ceremonies in 1933 and for many years participated in Hopi dances that were performed every evening for the tourists. Pemauhye carved and sold kachina dolls and was the subject of a postcard photograph.

During much of his time at the Grand Canyon, Pemauhye lived in a hogan located near Hopi House. He retired after forty-four years of employment around 1960 and returned home to the village of Shungopovi.

✦ FRED KABOTIE ✦

BORN AROUND 1900 in the Hopi village of Shungopovi, Fred Kabotie would travel away from his home on many occasions for months or years at a time, but would always return home. During some of the periods away from home, Kabotie worked for the Fred Harvey Company giving tours, painting murals, and managing the gift shop at Hopi House.

Kabotie's paintings also came to the attention of Harvey Company employees and were collected by J. F. Huckel and Mary Jane Colter. In the late 1920s, Colter decorated La Fonda Hotel in Santa Fe with Native American paintings on behalf of the Harvey Company. The Harvey Company was also selling paintings at the Indian Building at The Alvarado Hotel in Albuquerque by 1930. Two of Kabotie's paintings were included in a Harvey Company-organized exhibition at the Nelson-Atkins Museum in Kansas City, Missouri, in 1934.

Fred Kabotie received many honors in his lifetime and exhibited paintings widely. As early as 1933, his paintings were included in a national exhibit, the

Exposition of Indian Tribal Arts, Inc., which was shown in a number of cities including Philadelphia, Buffalo, Boston, and at the Cocoran Gallery in Washington, D. C. In 1945, Fred Kabotie was awarded a Guggenheim Fellowship. He died in 1986.

Fred Harvey's grandson Frederick Harvey and Fred Kabotie stand near the murals Kabotie painted at the Watchtower, 1933.

At the close of the last speach, which will perhaps be by Mr. Mather, Mr. Peters or some one will introduce Hopi Joe [Joe Secakuku] who will speak for a minute or two in Hopi. His speach will presumably be a repetition of the information I obtained by careful questioning while Mr. Peters made notes.

After Hopi Joe finishes his talk, Mr. Peters or Mr. Mather or some one will step forward and render in English a version of this information a copy of which you will find last attached herewith. At the conclusion of this talk, the six other Hopis, who will in the meanwhile be brought up the back stairway, will step forward in line facing the audience in the main lobby. After the Hopis are in position, the speaker will make an announcement about as follows: "Our Hopi friend and his brothers will now chant a prayer to the Katchina, their gods, that the hopes here expressed may be fulfilled, and I may add that this is a sacred invocation and one of the Hopis most ancient prayer."

At this stage, at a signal from the speaker, all lights in the lobby will go out with the exception of one lamp directly over the Indians who will sing standing accompanied by the low rumbling of a drum. At the close of the song and return of the lights, the Hopis will retire by the back stairs, the speaker will again step forward making announcement about as follows:

"Our Indian friends will now, to conclude this ceremony, entertain you by rendering a few songs and dances; . . . the same no doubt as witnessed by Del Tovar and his men when they discovered this Canyon four hundred years ago. Step right out in front of the hotel, take your time, there is room for all."

It has been planned to have a small camp fire in the middle of the drive in front of the hotel, the dancers performing around this fire; a dancing radius of about twenty-five feet will be kept clear. The hotel porch and steps will form one side of a sort of amphitheatre. The balance of the circle will be completed with railroad ties and planks; ushers will be designated to properly distribute the audience.

All the Indian women and children will be seated (dressed in their best) in a massed group on one side of the circle and facing the hotel entrance. When the audience starts out of the lobby, their eyes will be met by this group and facing a camp fire by the side of

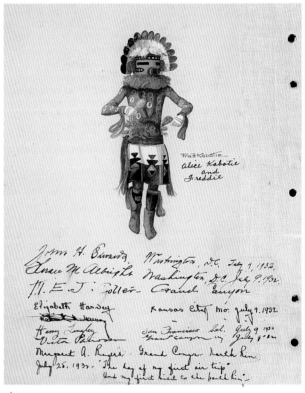

This guest book page, 1932, from the home of Grand Canyon National Park Superintendent M. R. Tillotson contains a watercolor by Fred Kabotie and signatures by Harvey family members and Mary Jane Colter.

which a single Navajo will be singing and beating a drum. This will insure continued action while the Hopis are coming down the back stairway and around the hotel.

P.S. Attached is the version of information obtained from the Hopis. This was written up hurriedly and may be cut down or enlarged as may be desirable.

It was around this same time that Hopi artist Fred Kabotie began a working association with the Harvey Company. As an adolescent, Kabotie attended the Santa Fe Indian School where he was encouraged to paint by the school superintendent's wife, Elizabeth DeHuff. After his school years, Kabotie kept in touch with the DeHuffs and would occasionally accompany Mrs. DeHuff on tours when she worked for the Harvey Company as a courier. By 1926 Elizabeth DeHuff was working for the Harvey Company Indian Detours as a courier and Kabotie may have been informally working for them. In his autobiography, Kabotie recalled accompanying DeHuff on tours:

Mrs. DeHuff gave lectures at La Fonda about the Indians and the country around Santa Fe. Sometimes when they'd have special visitors who had their own cars, Mr. DeHuff would call on me to guide them around Santa Fe and even take them up to Taos. . . . When I'd get back to Santa Fe with my visitors, we'd usually know each other well enough that they'd buy one of my paintings and pay me for the trip.

Kabotie developed a formal working relationship with the Fred Harvey Company in the 1920s when he was hired along with Porter Timeche and others to give telescope tours to visitors to the Grand Canyon. In 1933 Kabotie was hired by Mary Jane Colter to paint murals on the interior walls of the "Hopi room" on the second floor of the Watchtower at Desert View at the Grand Canyon.

Plans for the Watchtower began in 1931 when Colter traveled by small plane to the Four Corners area to research prehistoric towers for the design of the Watchtower. Herman Schweizer traveled with Colter's small party. By now Schweizer and Colter had each been with the Harvey Company for thirty years. Both had strong personalities and shared an abiding interest in Southwestern history and culture. Colter recorded her visits to gather information for the project.

PORTER TIMECHE

AFTER ALMOST FIFTY YEARS OF SERVICE, Porter Timeche retired from employment with the Fred Harvey Company at the Grand Canyon in 1970. Timeche left his home in the Hopi village of Shungopovi in 1924 and began working at Hopi House at the South Rim. He was hired to demonstrate blanket weaving to visitors along with basketweavers, silversmiths, and potterymakers. His first job lasted only about a month, during which time Timeche discovered that he was removing as many yarns as he was weaving as visitors repeatedly requested him to show them what he had done so that they might understand the weaving process. Timeche was discouraged that he would be unable to earn ample money since he could not weave many blankets. When he attempted to quit the job, however, he was offered a position as salesman at the gift shop at Hopi House.

Timeche was engaged in many interesting experiences while employed by the Harvey Company. In 1948, he helped to run the Santa Fe Indian Village at the Chicago Railroad Fair. While in Chicago, he was interviewed by a local radio station. In 1965, he was made an honorary airline captain at ceremonies marking the opening of the new airport near the South Rim. During the last twenty-three years of his employment, Timeche served as a buyer for the Harvey concessions at the Grand Canyon.

Porter Timeche, fourth from right, and Hopi Eagle dancers at the Watchtower dedication in 1933.

OPPOSITE:

*Jack Timeche in the gift shop at
the Watchtower, 1930s*

Photographs illustrate visits to sites of Cliff Palace and Cedar Tree Tower at Mesa Verde National Park, Hovenweap, Aztec Ruin, and other sites. Information collected during this Four Corners trip formed the basis for the design, building, and decoration of the Watchtower.

The Watchtower is seventy feet tall and thirty feet at the base. A steel framework, made by the bridge department of the Santa Fe Railway, was surrounded by the stones of the tower walls. Stones from the surrounding region were carefully selected by shape to form the walls. The ground floor contains a large, round room with a spectacular view of the Canyon. Narrow stairways led to upper floors where the murals painted by Fred Kabotie could be viewed.

The dedication of the Watchtower took place May 13, 1933, accompanied by all the publicity and fanfare that had ushered in the openings of the Alvarado, El Tovar, and El Navajo hotels, and other Harvey Company edifices. Fred Kabotie and Peter Nuvamse were asked to organize a group of Hopi people to come from the villages and present dances.

Colter developed a 100-page handbook for guides of the Watchtower titled *Manual for Drivers and Guides Descriptive of the Indian Watchtower at Desert View and Its Relation, Architecturally, to the Prehistoric Ruins of the Southwest*. The handbook provides the history of Southwestern prehistoric ruins.

Kabotie continued a working association with the Harvey Company as shop manager at Hopi House from 1935 until 1937. He was hired to paint murals for the Harvey Company's newly established Painted Desert Inn near Holbrook in 1947, and his final employment with the Harvey Company was to paint murals in the Bright Angel cocktail lounge in the 1950s.

CHAPTER 9

HARVEY COMPANY TOURS

I was a little girl when the buses were coming in. . . . They looked like long cars to me. . . . Maybe the adults knew when the buses were coming but it felt to me like something just happened everywhere at once and then people would start coming out of their houses with their pots in baskets which were wrapped in white dishcloths. . . . They'd sit on the ground, first kneel on the ground to open their baskets, it was always done with such humility.
—RINA SWENTZELL, *Santa Clara Pueblo, Age 56, 1995*

Watercolor of Harvey girl by F. J. Hinchman, 1920s

OPPOSITE
Harveycars at the Grand Canyon, 1920s

The Fred Harvey Company provided guided tours from many of the scenic spots both near and far from the railroad tracks. In addition, Harvey employees such as Schweizer and Huckel acted as host and guide for important guests to the Southwest. Schweizer, in a three-page letter to Huckel in 1917, tells of the ordeal of a trip to Keams Canyon. Six feet of snow had fallen between the time Schweizer left Albuquerque and arrived in Holbrook. The car in which he was riding broke down and was repaired by a black-smith who worked until midnight. The weather turned cold and he was stranded in Holbrook for a day. Continuing with his driver:

Harvey Couriers, 1920s; from left:
Farona W. Konopak, Mary Tucker,
Hazel Miller, and Margaret W. Moses.

Two miles further on there was a creek which had risen and although it was five below zero, the water was running pretty swift: we got stalled right in the middle of it. Shortly afterwards it got dark and the chauffeur and I after waiting a couple of hours had to leave the car and wade across the creek ourselves as we would have frozen to death if we would have stayed there any longer. We finally reached the Indian camp shortly after the mechanic arrived. The chauffeur went back with the horses, but they could not pull the car out and broke the chains. About 9 o'clock they returned and the chauffeur and the mechanic walked ten miles through the snow to Holbrook. They got back to the Indian camp about 3:30 in the morning and took me into town. Outside of that I had a pretty good trip.

On another occasion, Schweizer wrote Ford Harvey of his conversation with King Gillette, the razor magnate, about the difficulty Gillette had in getting to the Snake Dance at Oraibi. He was involved in a traffic jam with twenty-five other cars and missed the ceremony. Ford Harvey penned a note across the bottom of the page and sent it back to Schweizer: "I always said this snake dance trip is a hard one."

In another travel story, Schweizer was faced with the breakdown of his automobile while driving on the reservation. Schweizer solved the problem by purchasing a vehicle traveling in the opposite direction and using the parts from it to repair his car. A lengthy explanation of his expense report for the month was forwarded to Huckel.

Actual guided tours for Santa Fe Railway passengers began as wagon excursions to the Grand Canyon. By 1915, increased automobile travel brought many tourists to the Canyon who could undertake the venture by personal car, but many of the rim roads were yet to be paved and some sites such as Hermit Rim and Yavapai Point were accessible only by wagon.

Harveycars provided seven different tours of the Grand Canyon in 1915 ranging from thirteen to sixty-six miles for the expense of a few dollars. Tour drivers expounded upon the history of the area as they covered the Canyon routes.

In New Mexico, daily trips were possible from Lamy to Santa Fe as early as 1916. No extra charge was assessed to Santa Fe Railway passengers who chose to travel the eighteen-mile trip on the spur line which was a separate track connecting the main line to Santa Fe. Harvey Company accommodations were available at the DeVargas Hotel—now called the Hotel St. Francis. A 1916 brochure promised passengers an encounter with people from other cultures:

> *The unique adobe flat-roofed houses; the quaint crooked streets; the burros loaded with wood; the mingling of the Indian and Spanish-speaking native and the frontiersman, and the many evidences of ye olden days on every side.*

Harvey Company organized tours increased and intensified under the leadership of Major R. Hunter Clarkson, a Scotsman who moved to the United States in 1920. Shortly after immigrating, Clarkson became employed by the Harvey Company and was appointed as head of transportation at the Grand Canyon. By 1925, and with approval from Ford Harvey, Clarkson had developed plans for more extensive tours. After some discussion the newly planned tours were called "Indian Detours."

The Harvey Company's Indian Detours encouraged tourists to step off transcontinental trains for a few days to travel by Harveycar, automobile, or bus to the surrounding Pueblo and

MARGARET TAFOYA

TODAY'S MATRIARCH OF SOUTHWESTERN pottery, Margaret Tafoya was born in the village of Santa Clara Pueblo, a frequently visited locale for the Harvey Company's Indian Detours.

Santa Clara Pueblo is well known for the polished black and red pottery made in the  village. At times the pottery is carved with deep incised designs and at other times decorated with an impressed line forming a bear claw design. The pottery made by Margaret Tafoya and generations of her family members is outstanding because of the high sheen achieved by polishing the unfired pottery with a smooth stone.

Some of the pottery made by Margaret Tafoya, her mother Sara Fina, and her sisters was purchased by the Harvey Company and remains in the collection at the Heard Museum. Margaret Tafoya recalls making small pottery sugar bowls and creamers to sell for use in the Harvey Company's La Fonda Hotel in Santa Fe, New Mexico.

These people [tourists] would look and every once in awhile they'd pick up something but in a strange way I think they were interested in us, too. But nobody ever really looked at each other. It was a strange, strange encounter.

—RINA SWENTZELL, *Santa Clara Pueblo, Age 56, 1995*

Spanish villages, prehistoric ruins, and spectacular landscapes of New Mexico, Colorado, and Arizona. The first buses, purchased from the Yellow Coach Company of Chicago, seated up to twenty-five people. Harvey Company family members, which included Frederick Harvey among others, as well as a few company employees, made the inaugural trip on December 15, 1925.

In 1926, the Harvey Company purchased Koshare Tours, a business Erna Fergusson had formed with Ethel Hickey in 1921. Fergusson's bachelor's degree from the University of New Mexico and Master of Arts degree in history from Columbia University in New York more than qualified her to provide tours of the Southwest. The Harvey Company employed Fergusson to train young women who came to be called "Couriers," to lead the tours.

> *If you haven't met these clever Couriers, you have a treat coming! They'll amaze you with sparkling facts about everything you see! They chatter Spanish or even Indian when the occasion arises. It's very helpful! They know their mountain heights and mesa widths and things too fierce to mention!"* (Ho! Let's Explore! *promotional brochure, 1930s*)

Young, educated women, well versed in a knowledge of the Southwest, were interviewed to serve as couriers. Fergusson trained couriers to provide interpretive information along the Indian Detour route. The rigorous training program included attending classes taught by prominent ethnologists and historians such as Dr. Edgar L. Hewett, director of the School of American Research in Santa Fe; Dr. A. V. Kidder, an archaeologist at Andover Academy; F. W. Hodge, staff member of the Museum of the American Indian in New York; and Charles F. Lummis, author and founder of the Southwest Museum in Los Angeles.

To the Indian people living in Detour destinations, tourists bearing cash and cameras brought with them both a welcome outlet for goods and a perhaps less welcome invasion of privacy. Women, especially potters, sold their handmade objects directly to the tourists.

> *[The Fred Harvey Company] used to bring in tourists. . . . When the Harvey bus came in we would take our pottery and spread it out, sell it. It was Gia's [her grandmother, Gia-Khun's] pottery.*

[During the Fred Harvey bus tour times] they were making pottery to make a living and mostly to feed their children, feed the family.

Christina's father used to have lots of little children and they would dance. He would gather up little children and they would dance for the Fred Harvey buses and they would dance every Sunday. He would have all those little boys dancing. Once in a while you'd see older people dancing for them.

There were a lot of Fred Harvey buses coming in, later when the cars started coming in they stopped the Fred Harvey buses.
—ROSE NARANJO, *Santa Clara Pueblo, Age 79, 1995*

Harveycars, drivers, and couriers, 1929

Pueblo pottery underwent changes along with the pueblo community. Pots that were made for household utensils were sold to collectors like the Harvey Company and other shop owners such as Candelario in Santa Fe. The Harvey Company prized the older, large ceramics, retaining many in the museum collection. But tourists needed to travel light and preferred the smaller pottery forms.

A major transition occurred in pueblo pottery in the early part of the twentieth century as objects made for home use were purchased extensively by outsiders and replaced by commercial goods. Hundreds of Native American–made baskets, pottery, and textiles were purchased from single villages by traders and ethnographers. Trading posts offered metal pots, pans, clothing, and other goods that easily replaced these handmade crafts. Simultaneously, as the non-native population of the region grew, the economics of Native inhabitants was affected. It was now necessary for Native people to purchase foods formerly grown or hunted. Cash or objects of barter were essential to the ever-increasing, cash-based economy.

Before the Harvey buses came it was hard for the women. After they started coming it seemed like the women were the ones who were the providers, the moneymakers, and the men did their farming. . . . Children would run to the buses. [The tourists] brought candy and sometimes apples and gave them to the children.
—GREGORITA
CHAVARRIA
age 89, Santa Clara Pueblo, 1994

Pueblo women were active participants in securing money for the household. Native men sought wage-earning jobs, many of them working for the Santa Fe Railway in Winslow or in California. Women took clay that had been fashioned into objects for home use for centuries and transformed the utilitarian pots into small objects that were now purchased as mementos of travels by American tourists. Pottery shapes also began to reflect objects in American culture such as candlesticks, sugar bowls, and creamers.

Tourists poured into Pueblo communities with great interest. The Harvey Company responded by delivering tours to the villages on feast days or by arranging scheduled dances for tourists' viewing pleasures. Tourist visits reduced privacy in Native communities and resulted in encounters that were frequently based on curiosity. The impact of these visits was seen from a variety of perspectives. For many pueblo residents, the encounters were an opportunity to sell their wares and a chance to display a sample of pueblo life to visitors. To others, the idea of being on display was invasive:

> *I think one of the more devastating things that Fred Harvey. . . . I got this real sense coming through me about how I felt, the feelings I had even as a child watching the buses coming in, the feeling of—we were not good enough, ourselves as people were not good enough, everything about us was not good enough. And here these people were coming in from . . . I think I just picked it up from everybody around me, the adults, the whole community. It was taking away our sense of self. It was not giving us any sense of pride because we were making pottery.*

ABOVE: *Harveycar at Santa Clara Pueblo, 1920s.* OPPOSITE: *San Ildefonso jar by Tonita Pena or Marianita Roybal, 10", c. 1920*

Blackware pottery, 10", from Santa Clara Pueblo, early 1900s. The jar on the right was made by Tomasita Tafoya Narenjo

RIGHT
Blackware jar, 19", by Margaret Tafoya, c. 1925

It didn't leave us with something special and something really incredibly beautiful but it was exposure to that other world, exposure to money, exposure to that other world made us feel less than adequate.

We were made to feel totally devalued. As money was becoming valued, our culture, ourselves, our way of life was devalued.
—RINA SWENTZELL, *Santa Clara Pueblo, Age 56, 1995*

Whether a demonstration of pueblo life or an invasion of privacy, the Harvey Detours were key to the Pueblos financial well-being. Sales of arts and crafts to visitors was an important source of cash as the pueblos adjusted to twentieth-century economics.

Although the Harvey Company's Indian Detours ceased operation in 1931, the automobile had made possible an intimate kind of tourist experience. By later decades, the invasion grew to such proportions that pueblo governments found it necessary to impose strict photography and behavior rules for visitors.

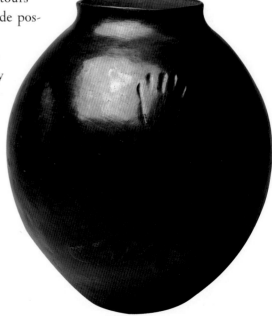

Untitled watercolor, 10 1/2" x 14", by Fred Kabotie, c. 1930. Harvey Company architect
Mary Jane Colter decorated the rooms at La Fonda with Native American paintings.

OFFICIAL EXHIBITOR
BOOTH NO: 430
NAME: Coyote & Rose
TRIBE: Coyote

CHAPTER 10

THE HARVEY COMPANY
LEGACY *in the* SOUTHWEST

"We've gone from ritual to retail." —EDMUND LADD, *Zuni Pueblo, 1994*

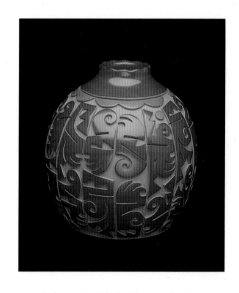

Redware jar, 14", by Tammy Garcia,
Santa Clara Pueblo, 1995

OPPOSITE
Coyote and Rose Doin' It At Indian
Market with a Little Help From Gail,
Yazzie, and Jody, *35" x 48", mixed media,*
by Harry Fonseca, 1982

The automobile burst upon the American scene, liberating individuals and families to travel on their own schedule. By 1919 nearly seven million automobiles were registered, and in that year alone an additional two million vehicles were built. Aided by federal government appropriations in 1916 and 1921, a national web of concrete and asphalt began to make inter-city auto travel quicker and safer. Each year in the 1920s, the United States spent a billion dollars or more to improve rural highways.

The completion of the transcontinental highway meant that the Santa Fe Railway no longer had a captive market. Travelers in their automobiles could select routes, places to stop and things to see on their own. A new roadside way of life emerged, dominated by filling stations, motels, cafés, and souvenir shops along the routes of U.S. 66 and other major highways. In 1922 the nation's first automobile-friendly shopping center, Country Club Plaza, opened its doors in the Fred Harvey Company's home town, Kansas City, Missouri.

I make pottery to make money, to make a living and pleasure. Making pottery takes a lot off your mind and it helps you to be patient, to relax sometime and, most of all, it's a joy to make it.
—ROSE NARANJO, *Santa Clara Pueblo, Age 79, 1995*

The Indian Department's businesses appear to have remained profitable until the Great Depression of the 1930s, when passenger traffic on the Santa Fe line began a steady decline. As more Americans chose to travel by automobile and airplane, the railroad hotels lost patronage. Ford Harvey died in 1928, J. F. Huckel in 1936, and Frederick Harvey, heir apparent and grandson of the founder, died in an airplane crash in 1933. The Harvey Company, the traveling public, and the market had changed.

In 1939, three years after Huckel's death, Fred Harvey's son, Byron Harvey, Sr., took over the reins of the Harvey Company. In a letter to Herman Schweizer on June 30, 1939, Byron Harvey, Sr., attempted to get Schweizer to reduce the Indian Department's inventory of old and expensive things:

> I am very much inclined to believe that we should exert ourselves more than I believe we are doing to sell some of the things you have in stock. I have in mind some of your rare and high-priced blankets and other things that in the past you have been able to handle to better advantage by keeping some in your vault and showing to a select few as they go through Albuquerque. With the new fast train schedules eliminating or cutting down the stop at Albuquerque, you have practically no opportunity now to handle these things as you used to be able to handle them and this situation probably will get worse instead of better. Another thing that worries me is that if anything happened to you, with your knowledge and particular ability in handling these things, I am afraid we would be under a very great handicap in disposing of same at anywhere near the prices that you could realize.

Apparently, Byron Harvey, Sr., was unable to persuade Schweizer to part with the collections it had taken forty years to amass. Schweizer could not bring himself to dispose of the collections after working so long and hard to find such fine and rare specimens. Consequently, a large portion of what was perhaps the finest collection of Indian art remained in the domain of the Fred Harvey Company. Ultimately, in 1978, these collections were donated to two museums in the Southwest: the Heard Museum in Phoenix received more than 4,000 art objects and the Museum of International Folk Art in Santa Fe received the balance of the collection.

By the 1960s, many of the company's facilities except those at the Grand Canyon and Death Valley were closed. However, Fred Harvey's name continues to be associated with hospitality and with hotels owned by other companies. The Harvey Company's influence persists in the Southwest today. The fair-like environment of Harvey Company establishments has given way to a spectrum of contemporary ventures ranging from actual theme parks to Indian Markets and museum-sponsored festivals and demonstrations. Santa Fe's Indian Market and the Gallup Inter-Tribal Ceremonial became annual events in the 1920s. Native American artists of the Southwest saw their work reach wider audiences through exhibits during the 1930s in New York and San Francisco. Fred Kabotie became, in 1945, the first Native American to be awarded a Guggenheim Foundation Fellowship.

In the 1980s, popular culture embraced the "Santa Fe Style" enthusiastically, broadening the mass market appeal of material culture originally brought to national attention by the Harvey Company's promotional activities. In the last quarter of the twentieth century, Native American arts reached a level of technical excellence. Many descendants of artists who worked for or sold to the Harvey Company, as well as other talented Native Americans, have created innovative works of art that share a heritage with the past.

The legacy of the combined efforts of the Santa Fe Railway and the Fred Harvey Company to promote and describe the Southwest—its peoples, their culture, and their home—thrives today. The tourist industry, one of the largest contributors to the economics of Arizona and New Mexico, is directly traceable to the ideals of hospitality fostered by the Fred Harvey Company. Our assumption of effortless travel among widely separated, remote destinations harkens back to the days of easy transportation by rail. Sustained promotions through advertising, publications, guided tours, world's

Tourism/Route 66 belt buckle, 1 1/2" x 3", by Gail Bird and Yazzie Johnson, 1995

OPPOSITE
*Polychrome jar, 11" diameter, by
Dextra Quotskuyva Nampeyo, 1985*

fair exhibits, and memorabilia alerted travelers to the attractions of one of America's most remote regions.

Ethnological research supported by the Harvey Company helped Americans of all backgrounds better understand the rich culture of many Native peoples. Collections assembled by the Harvey Company form the basis of several museums including the Heard Museum, the Nelson-Atkins Museum of Art, the Field Museum of Natural History, the Carnegie Museum of Natural History, the American Museum of Natural History, the National Museum of the American Indian, and the Museum für Völk-erkunde in Berlin. These collections reflect the diverse lives of Native Americans in the late 1800s and early 1900s.

Unwavering insistence by J. F. Huckel and Herman Schweizer that Native American–made objects purchased by the Indian Department be of the highest quality and best design set a high standard characteristic of Native American arts and crafts today. Family artistic traditions bearing the names of Nampeyo, Kabotie, Martinez, and many others nurtured by the Harvey Indian Department employment and exposure continue today through the creative efforts of children, grandchildren, and great-grandchildren.

Today's image of the Southwest—from the widely used thunderbird to the Grand Canyon, were developed, shaped, and brought forth to the minds of men and women of this country by the symbiotic promotion of railway and tourism. The Fred Harvey Company and the Atchison, Topeka, & Santa Fe Railway molded the image of the Southwest and presented it to the traveling public during the first half of this century.

RIGHT
*Polychrome jar, 13 1/2" diameter, by
Camille Quotskuyva Nampeyo, 1995*

Byron Harvey III

Byron Schermerhorn Harvey III was born on November 15, 1932, the great-grandson of Fred Harvey. Byron attended Harvard University and received a bachelor of arts degree from the University of Chicago in 1954. He continued his studies, earning a master of arts degree in anthropology from the University of New Mexico in Albuquerque in 1960.

As a young boy, Byron Harvey III acquired a keen interest in Native American objects that would influence his activities during his lifetime. His university studies and his personal friendships with Native Artists provided him with a broad knowledge of Native Peoples and the arts and crafts they produced. Byron began collecting as a boy. By 1956 he was actively building a personal collection from his home in Phoenix, Arizona. His collection has been featured in several publications, including *Hopi Painting: The World of the Hopis*, written by Patricia Jane Broder in 1978.

Byron Harvey III became a central figure who helped to shape the future of the corporate collection begun by the Harvey Company in 1902. In 1969 when the Fred Harvey Fine Arts Foundation was formed to oversee the activities of the Harvey Company collection, Byron Harvey III was an active member. In the 1960s and 1970s, he actively researched the collection that was housed at the Heard Museum and many other museums in the Southwest. Several articles were written by him in these early years. In 1963 he wrote "Masks in a Maskless Pueblo: The Laguna Colony Kachina Organization at Isleta," which was published in the magazine *Ethnology*. In 1970 *Ritual in Pueblo Art: Hopi Life in Hopi Painting* was published by the Museum of the American Indian, Heye Foundation (now the National Museum of the American Indian). In 1972, "An Overview of Pueblo Religion" was published in *New Perspectives on the Pueblos*, edited by Alfonso Ortiz, through the University of New Mexico Press, Albuquerque.

Through the years, Byron Harvey III gave generously of his personal object, archive, and photographic collections to museums throughout the United States including the Peabody Museum at Harvard University, the Field Museum in Chicago, the Museum of Northern Arizona in Flagstaff, and the Wheelwright Museum of the American Indian in Santa Fe. More than 2,000 objects have been donated to The Heard Museum by Byron Harvey III.

In 1978 Byron Harvey III served as a Harvey Company Foundation board member when more than 4,000 objects from the Fred Harvey Fine Arts collection were donated to The Heard Museum and a smaller collection was given to the Museum of International Folk Art in Santa Fe, New Mexico.

Byron Harvey III befriended and sponsored many Native American artists. In 1991 he was recognized for his outstanding contributions to the Native American community by the Phoenix Indian Center.

BIBLIOGRAPHY

Adair, John. *The Navajo and Pueblo Silversmiths.* Norman: University of Oklahoma Press, 1944.

Akin, Louis. Unpublished correspondence. Schaumburg, Illinois: Santa Fe Railway Archives, 1909.

Albuquerque Journal-Democrat. 1 March 1902–26 September 1903.

Albuquerque Morning Journal. 19 May 1904–8 August 1924

The Albuquerque Tribune. 4 January 1971.

Amsden, Charles Avery. *Navajo Weaving: Its Technic and History.* Albuquerque: The University of New Mexico Press, 1949.

Ashton, Robert. "Nampeyo: The Birth of Contemporary Hopi Pottery." *Southwest Art* 5, no. 2 (1976): 74–75.

Babbitt, Bruce E. *Color and Light: The Southwest Canvases of Louis Akin.* Flagstaff: Northland Press, 1973.

Babcock, Barbara A. "First Families: Gender, Reproduction and the Mythic Southwest." In *The Great Southwest of the Fred Harvey Company and the Santa Fe Railway.* Phoenix: the Heard Museum, 1996.

———. "Pueblo Cultural Bodies." *Journal of American Folklore* 107, no. 423 (1994): 40–54.

Babcock, Barbara A., and Nancy J. Parezo. *Daughters of the Desert.* Albuquerque: The University of New Mexico Press, 1988.

Bartlett, Karen, producer of the 1996 film, *Mary Jane Colter: House Made of Dawn.* Conversations with Kathleen L. Howard, 1994–95.

Birdseye, Roger W. "A Typical Spanish Rancho 'La Posada'." *The Santa Fe Magazine,* November 1930.

———. "Selling New Mexico Right." *New Mexico Highway Journal* 4, no. 9 (1926): 7–9.

Blomberg, Nancy J. *Navajo Textiles: The William Randolph Hearst Collection.* Tucson: University of Arizona Press, 1988.

Bol, Marsha. "Leave It to Cleaver": Collecting Symbolism Among the Arapaho." In *The Great Southwest of the Fred Harvey Company and the Santa Fe Railway.* Phoenix: the Heard Museum, 1996

Bowman, Leslie Green. *American Arts and Crafts: Virtue in Design.* Boston: Bulfinch Press, 1990.

Brugge, David M. *Hubbell Trading Post National Historic Site.* Tucson: Southwest Parks and Monuments, 1993.

Bunzel, Ruth. *The Pueblo Potter.* New York: Columbia University Press, 1929.

Candelario, Jesus Sito. Candelario Papers. Museum of New Mexico History Library, Santa Fe.

Chapman, Kenneth M., and Bruce T. Ellis. "The Line-Break, Problem Child of Pueblo Pottery." *El Palacio* 58, no. 9 (1951): 251–289.

Christmas Gifts [brochure]. Chicago: Fred Harvey, n.d.

Clark, Ann Nolan. "Frontier Grandeur." *New Mexico,* August 1935.

Cole Douglas. *Captured Heritage: The Scramble for Northwest Coast Artifacts.* Seattle: University of Washington Press, 1985.

Cole, Sally J. *The Abo Painted Rocks Documentation and Analysis, A Report Prepared for Salinas National Monument, New Mexico,* 1984. 8–12, 29, 40, Appendix 1. Unpublished. Copy obtained at Salinas National Monument.

Colter, Mary. *Manual for Drivers and Guides—descriptive—of The Indian Watchtower at Desert View and Its Relation, Architecturally, to the Prehistoric Ruins in the Southwest.* Grand Canyon National Park: Fred Harvey, 1933.

Colter, Mary E. J. Four photo albums, Vol I–IV. 1933. Fred Harvey, Indian Watchtower, Desert View. Grand Canyon National Park Museum Collection. Catalog No. 18642.

Collins, John E. *Nampeyo, Hopi Potter: Her Artistry and Legacy.* Fullerton, California: Muckenthaler Cultural Center, 1974.

Colton, Mary F. Russell, and Harold S. Colton. "An

Appreciation of the Art of Nampeyo and Her Influence on Hopi Pottery." *Plateau* 15, no. 3 (1943): 43–45.

Culin, Stewart. Field Report. New York City: Brooklyn Museum, 1907.

Davies, Cynthia, ed. *White Metal Universe: Navajo Silver from the Fred Harvey Collection.* Phoenix: the Heard Museum, 1976.

D'Emilio, Sandra, and Suzan Campbell. *Visions & Visionaries: The Art & Artists of the Santa Fe Railway.* Salt Lake City: Gibbs Smith, Publisher, 1991.

Dillworth, Leah. "Discovering Indians in Fred Harvey's Southwest." *The Great Southwest of the Fred Harvey Company and the Santa Fe Railway.* Phoenix: the Heard Museum, 1996.

Dorsey, George A. *Indians of the Southwest.* Passenger Department of the Atchison, Topeka & Santa Fe Railway System, 1903.

———. Unpublished correspondence. Chicago: Field Museum of Natural History, 1896–1915.

Eaggen, Fred. *Hopi Material Culture.* Phoenix: the Heard Museum, 1979.

Eldh, Don, owner of the Casteñeda Hotel 1995. Conversation with Kathleen L. Howard, Las Vegas, New Mexico, 22 August 1995.

[Elle] "Renowned Navajo Weaver Passes to Happy Hunting Ground." *The Santa Fe Magazine,* February 1924.

Fergusson, Erna. *Our Southwest.* New York and London: Alfred A. Knopf, 1940.

Fewkes, Jesse Walter. "Designs on Prehistoric Hopi Pottery." In *Thirty-third Annual Report of the Bureau of American Ethnology.* Washington: Smithsonian Institution, 1896.

First Families of the Southwest. Kansas City: Fred Harvey, 1915.

"Ford Ferguson Harvey," a chapter from an untitled, unpublished, undated manuscript in the private collection of Stewart Harvey, Boston.

Fred Harvey Blanket Ledgers. Phoenix: the Heard Museum.

Fred Harvey Company Correspondence. Phoenix: the Heard Museum Library and Archives.

Frisbie, Theodore R. "The Influence of J. Walter Fewkes on Nampeyo, Fact or Fancy?" In *The Changing Ways of Southwestern Indians: A Historical Perspective.* Glorieta, New Mexico: Rio Grande Press, 1973.

Gabriel, Kathryn. *Marietta Wetherill: Reflections of Life in Chaco Canyon.* Boulder: Johnson Books, 1992.

"The Grand Canyon of Arizona at the Panama-Pacific Exposition." *The Santa Fe Magazine,* July 1914.

Grattan, Virginia L. *Mary Colter: Builder Upon the Red Earth.* Grand Canyon: Grand Canyon Natural History Association, 1992.

Gruehl, Howard. "Tom and Elle—Navajos." *Illustrated World,* November 1922. 417–19, 466.

Harvey, Byron III. *The Fred Harvey Company Collects Indian Art.* Phoenix: the Heard Museum, 1981.

———. *The Fred Harvey Fine Arts Collection.* N.p., 1976.

———. "The Fred Harvey Collection, 1899–1963." *Plateau* 36 (1963): 33–53.

Harvey, Ford. Letter to Herman Schweizer. 21 March 1917. Fred Harvey Indian Department Correspondence. Phoenix: the Heard Museum.

Heard, Mrs. Dwight B. Letter to the Fred Harvey Company, Albuquerque, New Mexico, 1930. Phoenix: the Heard Museum Accession Records.

Hegemann, Elizabeth Compton. *Navajo Trading Days.* Albuquerque: University of New Mexico Press, 1987.

Hodge, Frederick Webb. "Death of Nampeyo." *Masterkey* 16, no. 5 (1942): 322–323.

Hough, Walter. "A Revival of the Ancient Hopi Pottery Art." *American Anthropologist* 19, no. 8 (1917): 322–323.

Howard, Kathleen L. "A Most Remarkable Success: Herman Schweizer and the Fred Harvey Indian Department." In *The Great Southwest of the Fred Harvey Company and the Santa Fe Railway.* Phoenix: the Heard Museum, 1996.

Howard, Kathleen L., and Marta Weigle. "Santa Fe Railway and Fred Harvey Publications, 1892–1930: A Selected Checklist."

The Great Southwest of the Fred Harvey Company and The Santa Fe Railway. Phoenix: the Heard Museum, 1996.

Hubbell, Dorothy. Interview by Kathleen L. Howard. Tape recording, 10 June 1988, Sun City, Arizona. Phoenix: the Heard Museum.

Huckel, J. F. Letters to J. L. Hubbell. 10 January, 26 April, 26 June, 20 July, 24 October, 1905. Hubbell Papers, Box 35. Special Collections. Tucson: The University of Arizona.

Hudson, John. John Hudson Papers. Grace Hudson Museum, Ukiah, California.

The Indian and Mexican Building [brochure]. Albuquerque: Fred Harvey, N.d.

Ivers, Louis Harris. "The Hotel Casteñeda, Las Vegas, NM: A Fred Harvey Inn on the Santa Fe Railway." NMA, May–June 1974.

Jacknis, Ira. "George Hunt, Collector of Indian Specimens." *Chiefly Feasts: The Enduring Kwakiutl Potlatch.* New York: American Museum of Natural History, 1991.

James, George Wharton. *Indian Blankets and Their Makers.* Chicago: A. C. McClurg & Company, 1918.

Judd, Neil M. "Nampeyo, An Additional Note." *Plateau* 24, no. 2 (1951): 92–93.

Kabotie, Fred, and Bill Belknap. *Fred Kabotie: Hopi Indian Artist.* Flagstaff: Museum of Northern Arizona with Northland Press, 1977.

Kansas City Times. 27 March 1936.

Kramer, Barbara. "Nampeyo, Hopi House and the Chicago Land Show. *American Indian Art Magazine* 14, no. 1 (1988): 46–53.

Lang, Anne M. Letter to Mr. Fred Harvey, Albuquerque, New Mexico. 1 August 1910. Fred Harvey Indian Department Correspondence. Phoenix: the Heard Museum.

Las Vegas Age. 19 March 1927.

Llamas, Michelle. "The Casteñeda Hotel: A Remnant of the Past." *The New Mexican,* 28 June 1974.

MacBride, Roger Lea, ed. *West From Home: Letters of Laura Ingalls Wilder to Almanzo Wilder, San Francisco 1915.* San Francisco: Harper & Row, 1965.

M'Closkey, Kathy. "Marketing Multiple Myths: The Hidden History of Navajo Weaving." *Journal of the Southwest* 36, no. 3 (1994): 186–220.

Marriott, Alice. *Maria: The Potter of San Ildefonso.* Norman and London: The University of Oklahoma Press, 1948.

Mather, Christine. *Colonial Frontiers: Art & Life in Spanish New Mexico, The Fred Harvey Collection.* Santa Fe: Museum of International Folk Art, 1983.

McClendon, Sally. "Collecting Pomoan Baskets, 1889–1939. *Museum Anthropology* 17, no. 2 (1993): 49–60.

McNitt, Frank. *Richard Wetherill: Anasazi.* Albuquerque: University of New Mexico Press, 1957.

———. *The Indian Traders.* Norman: University of Oklahoma Press, 1962

[Montezuma] "A Brief History of the Montezuma Hotel." N.d. Las Vegas: The Armand Hammer World College of the American West.

[Montezuma] *Hot Springs: Las Vegas, New Mexico* [brochure]. [Chicago:] Passenger Department Santa Fe Route, 1901.

[The] Montezuma. Hanging files in the Las Vegas Public Library. Las Vegas, New Mexico.

Las Vegas Daily Optic, 6 May 1992.

San Diego Historical Society. Newsreel footage, 1915. The Painted Desert Exhibit at the Panama-California Exposition in San Diego.

The Painted Desert Exposition: San Diego Exposition [1915 brochure]. Museum of New Mexico History Library. Santa Fe, New Mexico.

Pardue, Diana. "The Fred Harvey Company: Patron of Native American Art and Artists." Paper presented at the Native American Art Studies Association Conference. Santa Fe, New Mexico, September 1993.

———. "Marketing Ethnography: The Fred Harvey Company and

George A. Dorsey." In *The Great Southwest of the Fred Harvey Company and the Santa Fe Railway*. Phoenix: the Heard Museum, 1996.

Pardue, Diana, and Kathleen L. Howard. "Making Art, Making Money: The Fred Harvey Company and Native American Artisans." In *The Great Southwest of the Fred Harvey Company and the Santa Fe Railway*. Phoenix: the Heard Museum, 1996.

Peterson, Susan. *The Living Tradition of Maria Martinez*. Tokyo, New York and San Francisco: Kodansha International, 1981

Peters, Kurt M., Assistant Professor at California State University, Sacramento. *Watering the Flower: The Laguna Pueblo and the Santa Fe Railroad, 1880-1943*. Manuscript.

Polling-Kempes, Lesley. *The Harvey Girls Women Who Opened the West*. New York: Paragon House, 1989.

Powell, Lawrence Clark. *Books West Southwest Essays on Writers, their Books and their Land*. Los Angeles: Ward Richie Press, 1957.

———. *Southwestern Book Trails: A Reader's Guide to the Heartland of New Mexico and Arizona*. Albuquerque: Horn & Wallace Publishers, 1963.

"The President's Blankets." *McKinley County Republican*, 30 April 1903.

Reichard, Gladys A. *Navajo Medicine Man*. New York: Dover Publications, 1977.

The San Diego Union. 24 March 1914.

The Santa Fe New Mexican. 13 June 1933.

Sargent, Homer. Collection Notebooks,1902–1914. Phoenix: the Heard Museum Library and Archives.

Schweizer, Herman. Letters to J. L. Hubbell. Hubbell Papers, Box 36. Tucson: Special Collections, The University of Arizona.

———. Letter to William Randolph Hearst, Albuquerque. 31 December 1905. Fred Harvey Indian Department Correspondence. Phoenix: the Heard Museum.

———. Letter to J. F. Huckel. 18 December 1908. Fred Harvey Indian Department Correspondence. Phoenix: the Heard.

———. Letter to Mary Austin, Albuquerque. 12 April 1930. Fred Harvey Indian Department Correspondence. Phoenix: the Heard Museum.

———. Letter to Dr. Harold Colton. 31 October 1942. Flagstaff: Museum of Northern Arizona Library.

———. Fred Harvey Company Correspondence. Phoenix: the Heard Museum.

"William H. Simpson Passes On, Death Claims the Head of the Santa Fe's Advertising Department After More Than Half a Century of Highly Constructive Service." *The Santa Fe Magazine*, July 1933.

Simpson, William. Letter to J. F. Huckel. 21 October 1929. "Descriptive Names for Santa Fe Trains, Pullman Equipment" file. Schaumburg, Illinois: Santa Fe Railway Archives.

———. Letter to Ford F. Harvey. 11 December 1918. "Descriptive Names for Santa Fe Trains, Pullman Equipment" file. Schaumburg, Illinois: Santa Fe Railway Archives.

Smith-Ferri, Sherrie. "The Harvey Company and Pomo Collection." In *The Great Southwest of the Fred Harvey Company and the Santa Fe Railway*. Phoenix: the Heard Museum, 1996.

———. "Basket Weavers, Basket Collectors, and the Market: A Case Study of Joseppa Dick." *Museum Anthropology*, June 1993.

Seymour, Tryntje. *When the Rainbow Touches Down*. Phoenix: the Heard Museum, 1987.

Sotheby's Fine American Indian Art [auction catalogue]. November 28, 1989.

Sunday Chicago Record Herald. 8 May 1903.

Thomas, D. H. *The Southwestern Indian Detours: The Story of the Fred Harvey/Santa Fe Railway experiment in "detourism."* Phoenix: Hunter Publishing Company, 1978.

Toya, Debra Haaland. "Memories of a Boxcar Village." *New Mexico Magazine*, August 1995.

Twitchell, Ralph Emerson, ed. *The Leading Facts of New Mexico*

History. Vol 5. Cedar Rapids, Iowa: The Torch Press, 1917.

Verkamp, Margaret. "History of Grand Canyon National Park." M.A. Thesis, Department of History, University of Arizona, 1940. Reprint, Grand Canyon Pioneers Society Collectors Series Vol. 1. Flagstaff: Grand Canyon Pioneers Society, 1993.

Voth, Henry R. Correspondence. Chicago: Field Museum of Natural History.

Wade, Edwin L. "The History of the Southwest Indian Ethnic Market." Ph.D. Diss., Seattle: University of Washington, 1977.

_____. "The Thomas Keam Collection of Hopi Pottery: A New Typology." *American Indian Art Magazine* 5, no. 3 (1980): 55–61.

_____. "The Ethnic Art Market in the American Southwest." In *Objects and Others: Essays on Museums and Material Culture.* Madison: University of Wisconsin, 1985.

_____. *The Arts of the North American Indian: Native Traditions in Evolution.* New York: Hudson Hills Press, Inc., 1986.

Wade, Edwin L., and Leah McChesney. *Historic Hopi Ceramics: The Thomas V. Keam Collection of the Peabody Museum of Archaeology and Ethnology.* Cambridge: Peabody Museum Press, 1981.

Weigle, Marta. "From Desert to Disneyworld: The Santa Fe Railway and the Fred Harvey Company Display the Indian Southwest." *Journal of Anthropological Research* 45, no. 1 (1989): 115–137.

_____. "Exposition and Mediation: Mary Colter, Erna Fergusson, and the Santa Fe/Harvey Popularization of the Native Southwest, 1902–1940." *Frontiers,* 13, No. 3 (1992).

_____. "Insisted on Authenticity: Harveycar Indian Detours, 1925–1931. In *The Great Southwest of the Fred Harvey Company and the Santa Fe Railway.* Phoenix: the Heard Museum, 1996.

Weigle, Marta, and Kyle Fiore. *Santa Fe & Taos: The Writers, 1916–1941.* Santa Fe: Ancient City Press, 1994.

Weigle, Marta, and Kathleen L. Howard. "To Experience the Real Grand Canyon: Santa Fe/Harvey Panopticism, 1901–1935." In *The Great Southwest of the Fred Harvey Company and the Santa Fe Railway.* Phoenix: the Heard Museum, 1996.

The Williams News. 25 March 1905.

Willie, Paul. Interview by Kathleen L. Howard. Tape recording, translated by Kathleen Tabaha. Teec Nos Pos, Arizona, 14 July 1993.

Wyman, Leland C. *Navajo Sandpainting: The Huckel Collection.* Colorado Springs: The Taylor Museum, 1971.

Acknowlegments

John and Casey Adair, San Francisco

Becky Alexander and Mary Allely, The City of San Diego Public Library, San Diego

Margaret Anderson, Chicago

Louis Archer, Albuquerque

Barbara Babcock, Regents Professor and Director of the Program in Comparative Cultural and Literary Studies, The University of Arizona, Tucson

Karen Bartlett and Sean McLinn, Nemesis Productions, Los Angeles

Craig Bates, Curator, Yosemite National Park, California

Jonathan Batkin, Director, Wheelwright Museum, Santa Fe

Liz Bauer, Mesa Verde National Park, Colorado

D. Y. Begay, Scottsdale, Arizona

Bruce Bernstein, Chief Curator & Assistant Director, Museum of Indian Arts and Culture and Laboratory of Anthropology, Santa Fe

Paul Benicek, Curator, and Cathy Westphal, Vice President, Santa Fe Railroad, Schaumburg, Illinois

David Binkley, Curator of the Arts of Africa, Oceania and the Americas, Nelson-Atkins Museum, Kansas City, Missouri

Gayle Bird and Yazzie Johnson

Lorencita Bird and Evelyn Quintana, San Juan Pueblo, New Mexico

Nancy Blomberg, Curator and Head of the Department of Native Arts, Denver Arts Museum, Denver

Martha Blue, Lawyer, Flagstaff, Arizona

Marsha Bol, Associate Curator of Anthropology, Carnegie Museum of Natural History, Pittsburgh

Dot Brovarney, Curator, Grace Hudson Museum, Ukiah, California

Tim Burch, Santa Fe

Thomas W. Burch and Shannon Morrow, The Raton Museum, Raton, New Mexico

Carol Burke, Museum of Northern Arizona, Flagstaff

Martha Clevenger, Archivist, Missouri Historical Society, St. Louis

Shalice Clinkscales, Photo Archivist, National Museum of the American Indian, New York City

Ruth and Aaron Cohen, Guidon Books, Scottsdale, Arizona

Chris Coleman, Collections Manager, Anthropology, Natural History Museum of Los Angeles County, Los Angeles

Scott Cutler, The Centennial Museum, University of Texas at El Paso

Dorothy Davis, Midland, Texas

Sharon Deen, Photo Archivist, National Museum of the American Indian, New York City

Joseph and Alberta Ernst, Scottsdale, Arizona

Maxine Edwards, Curator, Arizona State Capitol Museum, Phoenix

Kathy and Don Fiero, Mesa Verde National Park, Mesa Verde, Colorado

Catherine Fowler, University of Nevada, Reno

Darrell Garwood, Audio Visual Archivist, Manuscript Dept., Kansas State Historical Society, Topeka

Vern Glover, Santa Fe

Cavan Gonzales (Tse-Whang), San Ildefonso Pueblo, Santa Fe

Rayna Green, Director, American Indian Program, National Museum of American History, Washington, D.C.

Janice Griffiths, Old Trails Museum, Winslow, Arizona

Douglas J. Hamilton, Tucson

Margaret Hardin, Curator, Los Angeles Museum of Natural History, Los Angeles

Deborah Harding, Registrar, Carnegie Museum of Natural
    History, Pittsburgh

Michael Harding, Rooms Director, Fred Harvey, Grand Canyon
    National Park Lodges, Grand Canyon

Betty-Mae Hartman, Albuquerque

Byron Harvey III, Cambridge, Massachusetts

Daggett Harvey, Jr., Chicago

Stewart Harvey, Boston

Michael J. Herring, Director, Indian Arts Research Center,
    School of American Research, Santa Fe

William G. Howard, Jr., Scottsdale, Arizona

Wesley and Mary Hurt, Laurel, Maryland

Lynn Horiuchi, Oakland, California

Dorothy Hubbell, Sun City, Arizona

Colleen Hyde, Museum Technician, Grand Canyon
    National Park

Mary Ann Johnson, Librarian, The Field Museum of Natural
    History, Chicago

Allison Jeffreys, Archivist, National Museum of the American
    Indian, New York City

Alan Jutzi, The Huntington Library, San Marino, California

Michael Kabotie, Hopi Pueblo, Arizona

Bob and Marianne Kapoun, The Rainbow Man, Santa Fe

Belinda Kaye, Registrar, American Museum of Natural History,
    New York City

Loretta Barrett Keleher, Albuquerque

Michael Keleher, Albuquerque

Clara Kinlicheenie, Wheatfields, Arizona

Janice Klein, Registrar, Field Museum of Natural History,
    Chicago

Christine Leishow, Special Collections Library, University of
    Arizona, Tucson

Mary Jane Lenz, Curator, National Museum of Natural History,
    New York City

Clifford Lomaheftewa, Phoenix

Kathy M'Closky, York University, North York, Ontario, Canada

Corrilea McDonough, Albuquerque

Connie Menninger, Kansas State Historical Society, Topeka

Bruce McGee, McGees Gallery, Holbrook, Arizona

Sally McLendon, Professor of Anthropology, Hunter College,
    New York City

William H. Mullane, Special Collections, Cline Library,
    Northern Arizona University, Flagstaff

Helen Harvey Mills, Chicago

Carol Naille, Flagstaff, Arizona

Tessie Naranjo, Director of the Cultural Preservation Program at
    Santa Clara Pueblo, New Mexico

Shirley Newcomb, Gallup, New Mexico

Jeff Ogg, Indian Handicraft and Souvenir Buyer, Fred Harvey,
    Grand Canyon

Arthur Olivas, Photographic Archivist, Museum of New Mexico,
    Santa Fe

Mo Palmer, Photo Archivist, The Albuquerque Museum,
    Albuquerque

Leslie Poling-Kempes, Abiquiu, New Mexico

Michael Quinn, Photo Archivist, Grand Canyon National Park

Dextra Quotskuyva Nampeyo and Camille Quotskuyva Nampeyo,
    Hopi Pueblo, Arizona

Al Regensberg, Senior Archivist, State of New Mexico Records
    and Archives Center, Santa Fe

Kathy Reynolds, Registrar, Colorado Springs Fine Arts Center,
    Colorado Springs

Mary Ann Rogers, Albuquerque

Richard Rudisill, Curator of Photographic History, Museum of
    New Mexico, Palace of the Governors, Santa Fe

Orlando Romero, Museum of New Mexico, History Library,
    Palace of the Governors, Santa Fe

Sherrie Smith-Ferri, Grace Hudson Museum, Ukiah, California

Diana and Joe Stein, Los Artisanos Books, Las Vegas

Jennie Stein, Chicago

Tom Stein, Libertyville

Kathleen Tabaha, Museum Technician, Hubbell Trading Post National Historic Site, Ganado, Arizona

Margaret Tafoya, Santa Clara Pueblo, New Mexico

Diane Thomas, Phoenix

Descheenie Nez and Rose Tracy, Ganado, Arizona

Cathy War, Archivist, University of Nevada Library, Las Vegas

Frank Waters, Taos, New Mexico

Jennifer Watts, Photo Archivist, The Huntington Library, San Marino, California

Marta Weigle, University Regents Professor of Anthropology and Chair of the Department of Anthropology at the University of New Mexico, Albuquerque

Sally West, Assistant Archivist, Coordinator Oral History Program, Museum of San Diego History, San Diego

Laile Williamson, Assistant Curator of North American Collections, American Museum of Natural History, New York City

Paul Willie, Teec Nos Pos, Arizona

Mark Winters, Pagosa Springs, Colorado

Kathy Wright, Acting Director, Colorado Springs Fine Arts Center, Colorado Springs

Index

Kathleen L. Howard is a research associate at the Heard Museum in Phoenix, Arizona. Her Heard activities focus on the museum's collection of the Fred Harvey Company papers; this led to her role as co-curator for *Inventing the Southwest: The Fred Harvey Company and Native American Art.* Prior to coming to the Heard, she wrote *A Guide to George Catlin's Souvenir of the North American Indians* at the Newberry Library in Chicago. She also served as co-project leader for the 1991 exhibit, *A Century's Perspective: Gustaf Nordenskiöld's Mesa Verde Today,* a centennial study of change at Mesa Verde National Park. Prior to her research activities, she was a purchasing agent with Motorola, Inc., in Phoenix, Arizona, and Schaumburg, Illinois.

Kathleen has a Bachelor of Science degree in Business Administration from Arizona State University. Her spare time is spent in boots and backpack exploring the back country of the Sonoran Desert and the Colorado Plateau.

Diana Pardue is curator of collections at the Heard Museum and is the lead curator for the Heard's *Inventing the Southwest* exhibit. In 1978, she became interested in the Fred Harvey Company collection when more than four thousand objects from it were donated to the Heard; she began to research the collection extensively in 1992 in preparation for an exhibit. Since 1978, when she began her work in the curatorial department at the Heard, Diana has served as curator for numerous exhibits, including *Chispas! Cultural Warriors of New Mexico* in 1992, *Generations of Traditions* in 1991, and *Earth, Hands, and Life: Southwestern Ceramic Figures* in 1988.

Diana received a Master of Arts degree in anthropology from Arizona State University in 1982 with a thesis topic of Western Apache beadwork. Her studies have given her a great appreciation of Southwestern arts and crafts and Native American artists. Her spare time is spent with her husband, Dan, and her ten-year-old daughter, Monica.